Christine Minogue is Australia's foremost Mothercraft Nurse with 30 years of experience in providing care and support for parents of newborns, infants and toddlers. Christine has been at North Shore Private Hospital for over 15 years (where she is currently an Antenatal Educator) and has a substantial private practice. Christine has a special interest in the first year of life, including multiple birth families.

Bringing
Baby Home

Christine
Minogue

MACMILLAN
Pan Macmillan Australia

Note: Throughout the book, in no particular order, I call your baby 'he' and 'she' or 'him' and 'her'. There is no set gender I have in mind when I'm talking about various things, especially discipline! It's only in preference to calling your baby 'it'.

First published 2016 in Macmillan by Pan Macmillan Australia Pty Ltd
1 Market Street, Sydney, New South Wales, Australia, 2000

Cataloguing-in-Publication entry is available
from the National Library of Australia
http://catalogue.nla.gov.au

Typeset design by Deborah Parry Graphics
Typeset in 13/17 pt Bembo by Post Pre-press Group, Brisbane
Printed by McPherson's Printing Group

The publishers and their respective employees or agents will not accept responsibility for injuries or damage occasioned to any person as a result of participation in the activities described in this book. It is recommended that individually tailored advice is sought from your healthcare professional.

I dedicate this to Mum and Dad for the gift of love,
for believing in me, encouraging me and allowing me to grow
into the person that I am today. Always in my heart.

CONTENTS

THE CHANGING FACE OF PARENTING

FOR as long as I can remember, I have been surrounded by babies. My youngest sister was born when I was eleven and I was helping and then babysitting a family of six from the age of thirteen. When other children brought home stray dogs and cats, I would be looking after and bringing home the neighbours' babies. I had a strong nurturing instinct; one that was developed from a young age and, I'm happy to say, has never wavered.

For most of my schooling, I thought I would grow up to be a policewoman or a paediatric nurse, but one day my maths teacher (probably tearing her hair out trying to teach me fractions) mentioned mothercraft nursing and that was it — I knew that's what I would be.

I graduated as a Karitane Mothercraft nurse in 1985 and since then my work has given me a career that has been as varied as it has been fulfilling. I've worked with children with disabilities and special needs at the Royal Far West Children's Hospital in Manly, Sydney, and taken trips around the world supporting families as they travelled, moved or brought their surrogate babies home. In 1990, after a short stint with day care nurseries, I started working in the private hospital sector until one day I realised there was a need to give mothers more support at home. I remember thinking, 'If only they knew what the baby really *needs*, it might make the task of being at home so much easier', so I started The Nurtured Way as a part-time business. Within six months it became my full-time job and to this day, twelve years later, it remains as busy as ever.

Now that I've been caring for young babies and their families for more than twenty-five years, I can look back and realise that, in that time, nothing and everything has changed.

As a child (and I didn't know it at the time), I was good at looking after other kids. I suppose it just felt very natural and therefore it wasn't hard. Now that I'm an adult I can see that the things that came naturally to me are what I discuss with new parents. The basic needs of children and parenting haven't really changed, what has changed is all the other 'stuff' that we live and deal with every day.

When I see parents for the first time, I usually ask the questions, 'How old is your baby and what is he or she doing?' and 'What do you think your child needs?'. Most parents tend to overthink it, wondering if I'm looking for a complicated answer. Sometimes parents just need to be reminded of a couple of things, and of course, being me, I don't hesitate to break it down like this:

Your child needs you for every second, of every minute, of every hour, of every day, of every week, of every month, of every year . . . until she is about twenty-five. Your child needs food, shelter, love and your time.

This might sound pretty dramatic when you're sitting there with your screeching infant and your urban warrior toddler, but the reality is, you've had a child or you have children, and they need you.

As for parents, there are so many styles of parenting. All families have differing needs. Some are overwhelmed and need bite-sized pieces of information so they can work through issues steadily. Others are really confident parents who need to break through the chaos of family life for some routine and peace. Most parents I meet want to know what their baby needs, not only for the baby's sake but to be able to function as a family.

There are always families that fall in and out of one or all of the above types, and we all know there is nothing binary about family life. The good news is that when I hear from parents, it always means they want to do the best they can for their family. And this is the greatest start you can give your family. If your child has your love, your time and your unwavering support, you will be fine. I'm here to help you through the chaos!

With the basics out of the way, I tend to believe there are issues that can cloud normally clear-thinking parents. These are the everyday challenges that most parents have to face and the decisions and consequences they have to deal with. I'm talking about work, parenting styles, social pressures and the ever-present internet virtually spewing out information on how to handle it all. It's exhausting and parents are often confused, overwhelmed, or both. When this happens, the basic nurturing instinct tends to get lost in all the noise, parenting becomes difficult and suddenly, that family life they dreamed about is a daily nightmare. My job is to cut through the noise, so to speak, and bring everyone back to the basics.

My book is about understanding your child's needs and how you can nurture your instincts to parent calmly. It isn't about routines (although I do offer my Cheat Sheets based on age-appropriate development) and it isn't a 'how to' book. You know what to do; you just need to allow yourself time and space to get to know your child and to keep a lid on those expectations! I will help you understand the basic needs of your children as they grow and what you can do to make sure their needs are met.

Mostly, though, I hope to help you to trust your instincts. It's okay to pick up your crying newborn and hold her close to you. And it's more than okay to spend your Sunday playing Lego in your pyjamas with your three-year-old. In my book, I make no bones about the difference between the dream and the reality of parenting. In fact, there's a whole chapter devoted to it. It's a wake-up call to the people who think that nothing will change once the baby is born and parenting begins when their child is a toddler.

Parenting can be wonderful and your children can delight you; it's just how you tackle it.

Chris Minogue

1

MUMS

THE first time I meet a woman to talk about her baby is usually either when she calls me to book a private antenatal class or shortly after her baby is born. This is mostly when the baby is her first. She does this because she has limited time to attend classes at the hospital and the baby is due imminently. She is thinking of all the work-related things she has to do before she has her baby and somewhere in amongst it all, having the baby is part of her list of Things To Do. Women like this are busy. Many of them have been working hard at a career and have jobs that are intellectually, physically and emotionally demanding. I also see women who are incredibly relaxed about having their first baby. I love meeting them all.

For a mum who is having another baby, however, there is a different agenda. She knows her baby needs time so the conversation I have with her is very different. She wants to know how she's going to manage the juggle of family life. Really, what she wants to know is when she needs to give structure to the baby's day and night, and/or how long can she get away with just dragging the baby along to all the things that she has going on, before it matters.

Every family's life is different. Granted, there are many similarities but you're all unique. In my antenatal classes, I try to focus on the fundamental aspect of life with a baby: that is, that babies need time. For busy mums – first baby or not – this cannot be stressed enough. You are going to have to adjust your life and your expectations so that when your baby arrives, you don't go into shock and denial about how much your life has changed. Get used to the idea that the rhythm of your life will change. No matter what your dream is, it *will* change and often in a way you least expect. The reality is, you have to simplify your life because that's what your baby needs. You can't function if you care for your baby twenty-four hours a day and keep up the pace of your pre-baby life. You can try it, but brace yourself.

This is the mindset I want you to move towards . . .

I'm not actually going to get a lot of sleep when this baby arrives. But that's okay, because my baby has spent the last nine months with food and comfort on tap. When my baby is born, she and I are going to have to get used to having each other around and that's going to take time. This weekend, I'm going to go out and buy a couple of pairs of comfy pyjamas or some on-trend loungewear (!) so I can settle into being at home. When friends and family want to catch up, I'll get them to come to me, via the supermarket.

I'm convinced mothers have a radar built into them — otherwise known as a sixth sense. Trust your instincts and get used to the relationship between you and your baby. Let people around you help you by feeding you and loving you and your baby. Take support so you can focus on making the transition to being a family. It does take time to adjust to this new life, and becoming a family involves all the emotions from joy, happiness and love to overwhelming fear and tiredness. All of this is normal but if fear, tiredness and despair persist, you need to speak up and get help.

2

DADS

LL the dads I've met want the best for their partner and children, and want, wherever possible, to be involved in family life.

These days, fathering is completely different to the generation my father knew. When I talk to grandparents in my classes, the men were mostly dads of young babies in the 1970s. The very heartening thing that I recognise between the men in the grandparents' class and dads of newborns today is that the grandfathers realise that their experience was very different. Most will say their role was traditional in the sense that they worked long hours outside the home and their wives cared for the children. Often I hear the phrase, 'I didn't really help out very much but I tried to at the weekend.' Today, dads are more overwhelmed by the prospect of parenthood because the community message is that not only can you go to work in a high-pressure job for twelve hours, but you can arrive home in the evening knowing exactly what to do with your children – no matter what they've been up to all day. This is unrealistic and unfair and I see a divide between the dads who will say of themselves, 'I'm completely hopeless, I just get my partner to tell me what to do', and dads who can take over the parenting for a week on their own without flinching.

Fathering needs to start with the pregnancy. It needs to begin with a good look at the reality of what's going to happen. Most importantly, there's going to be another human in the house. There could be more pressure on the single income for a while, at least. Late nights are likely to grind to a halt and weekends away with the lads might have to be cut back to a couple per year (!). As I write this, I'm thinking about dads in the city, because that's where most of my clients are, but it does get me remembering the families I've helped who live in the country. Those dads are just as busy and often spend long days (whenever there's daylight) out working on the property. They might come home for lunch if they're working near the house, but those days can be just as long, probably longer, than the days of their city counterparts. For country dads, there are opportunities for the kids to help on the farm and certainly as they grow older, this creates wonderful memories for families, particularly if mothers are getting out as well.

One of the big stressors for dads is their job. When we're sitting in an antenatal class, I'll ask the dads, 'How much time are you having off?' The range is between two and four weeks, which I'm always happy to hear. It's important for the whole family to have this time together. Initially, dads experience a sense of overwhelming responsibility. They see their partner in labour and their child being born and they think, 'Oh my Lord, look what *I* have to keep alive and functioning!' They feel hugely protective of both their partner and their child. They need time to get used to the idea of being a dad and definitely time to learn how to change nappies, wrap, cuddle and settle their baby. When they've returned to their job, this precious time will pay back in spades when a grumpy baby is thrust into dad's loving arms the minute he walks in the door.

There's another player in dad's life here who I haven't forgotten; mum. I see many, many mums who are the heart and soul of the family. They are left to their own devices, pretty much from a week after the baby is born, and they are amazing. The happy news is that, mostly, their partners cherish them and want to give them all the support they can. Mums, however, can become so independent that sometimes dads can feel like they are in the way. It's an issue that only communication and effort can resolve. Mum needs to resist telling dad how to do everything; yet dad needs to try not to be oversensitive if mum interjects when she can see the wheels are about to fall off. In short, you're both parents of your baby so you need to work together as best you can.

If I stand back and look at the dads I've met, most of them want to be part of the new baby's life. But reality sets in and they're working long days with an expectation that when they walk through the door at seven at night, they'll parent perfectly. Dads need to be gently nurtured into the role and that's about communication. There are fundamentals like settling, discipline, house rules and so on, but for the basics such as nappies and feeding patterns, mums can show how it's done and then step away. Being a hands-on father is about taking responsibility, and this matters! When you're taking care of your kids, you take responsibility for them – whether you're feeding them or taking them in the car to soccer training. Your kids are also seeing you share that responsibility with their mother, and that is a good thing. You're teaching them not only to kick a soccer ball or take their plate to the sink when they've finished eating, you are *showing* them how to have a fair and respectful relationship with another human. Your children are looking at the way you treat your partner and they are learning that if their father is respectful and mindful of their mother, then that is the way people should treat each other. If their father is distant, agitated and perhaps abusive in either a physical or a mental way, then that is how they see how relationships work.

I often ask dads, 'What do you want your child to be as a sixteen-year-old?' and the answer is usually something like, 'I want my child to be loving life, having fun, being respectful and mindful of others and being an overall good person'. The conversation always turns to the parents having to be the ones that are going to teach their child to love life, have fun, be respectful and mindful – to be a good person.

Let's look at the reality of the first few weeks with a newborn.

I suggest in the first few weeks you simply get used to things being different. If your partner has had a normal delivery and she and the baby are doing well, you would have had that first week in hospital or at home with lots of people around to help. When you get home, a day can be a long time. Your partner is recovering from the delivery; she's spending a lot of time feeding and settling the baby and resting between feeds. So what can you do to help? The best thing to do is to keep the rest of the house going and get to know your baby. If it's your first, you'll both be fumbling about with feeding, wrapping, bathing and settling. You will both be pretty tired – a feeling not unlike jet lag but it'll take about six weeks for you to get back to normal, longer if you're up at night feeding and longer still for your partner.

If you're going back to work in a couple of weeks, you'll need to sort out what you're doing each day and who is going to give your partner a hand when you're not there. What other support do you have? Try to set up a few systems that are going to work when you can't be around. It might mean setting up the online grocery list, organising a weekly fresh fruit and veg delivery, sorting out some help around the house with washing and cleaning. These things may not be permanent changes but they are going to be helpful for the next few months. Your partner will look forward to spending time with *you* when you get home, not the ironing board. You could do the paperwork needed after you have a baby – things like registering the birth, adding your baby's name to policies and so on. These are very useful activities and ones that can fall by the wayside when family life takes over!

Another very handy thing for dads to do is to keep 'the gallery' at bay. By 'gallery' I mean keeping the flow of visitors to a minimum. Though well meaning and usually great company, they always tend to arrive at a meal time and they're always hungry. You do *not* need to feed guests and your partner most certainly does *not* need to have them hanging around when she's trying to feed and settle the baby. Boiling the kettle for a quick cuppa at morning tea is all you need to offer. Learn to say no and put your partner and baby first. If they're friends worth hanging on to, they'll understand and they'll be back.

Despite the demands of home life, an important thing to remember when you're a dad is to keep in touch with your mates. Keep up the exercise; maybe just find an activity that doesn't take up two hours each day and every Saturday. Many dads tend to keep work issues and worries to themselves for fear of upsetting a fragile home life. This is admirable but not okay in the long run. Your partner is still interested in what you do – probably desperate to talk about something other than babies too – so share the load but perhaps pick your moments. If the moments are a bit few and far between, ring a mate and arrange to catch up. Other dads are fantastic to talk to – they've been through the same issues and if you feel you can, let them know if you're struggling. If things really feel like they're getting on top of you, make an appointment with your GP to have a chat. Bottling up issues simply builds resentment. It's the same with anything, except that with family, it builds. Just keep talking with your partner and try to keep as calm as you can. If you want to contribute or make a suggestion, do so; just don't turn it into an argument!

Readjusting to something that is permanent is a big deal. It's a commitment and one you can't take lightly. It's a commitment you make to your child, as well as your partner. You need to think about what you can commit to and how it's going to affect your family. I'm being realistic here because I have seen many families with *unrealistic* views about how much time they can commit to family.

Think about it this way: Are you going to work long hours during the week so that at the weekend you can commit to your family? If you're going to do this, what does your partner need in terms of support? Does she need help during the week? It might be a good idea to hire someone to clean or help out occasionally. I know of a family who paid their (retired and trusted) neighbour for two hours, twice a week, to take the baby out for a walk. This is a perfect opportunity for mums to have a break and get a haircut, read, sleep or simply have some baby-free time.

Tips for dads

There are a few little secrets I want to share with dads for when they go back to work.

- You need to get a good sleep at night in order to function at work so if you're able to, set up a bed in another room if you need better rest.
- If you're doing the above, remember that your partner may *not* be getting the sleep she needs so it is incumbent upon you to perhaps take on a greater share of her emotional load (this is tiring for you, but not nearly as tiring as it is for her).
- Before you leave for work, pull something out of the freezer for dinner and tell your partner you've got it covered.
- Just before you leave work, call home to see how your partner's afternoon has been; ask her to switch the oven on and throw in the now-thawed dinner you pulled out of the freezer that morning.
- When you get home, ask her where she's at with the baby and if she'd like you to take over.
- Try to resist collapsing on the couch and flicking on the television the minute you walk in the door – this could have a devastating effect on both of you.
- Be as positive as you can be without being glib.

- Hearing about baby poo and tiredness would be just as banal for your partner if you swapped roles and you were doing the talking, so get into it, have a laugh and enjoy the detail.
- Sitting down together for twenty minutes to talk is better than twenty one-minute soundbites – tune into each other and really listen – it's good for both of you.
- Enjoy being an involved and present dad. Your partner *does* need you and the effort and compromise you make in those early years will only make your family stronger.

3

SINGLE PARENTING

To me, single parents are amazing. There is no shortage of love; it's always just the juggle of managing alone. I have a number of single parent clients and each one sees their parenting not as a struggle but as a journey. They want to show their child that life and relationships exist outside their own family. I also see that once the busyness of the early years is over, particularly for those who have twins, they start to put time back into themselves. These parents are getting babysitters while they go out for dinner with friends; they go back to work either part- or full-time; and they might be open to meeting a partner. They have busy lives and you'd think the combination of work and parenting might make them want to say, 'That's enough', but they don't. They want to do things they enjoy and, by doing so, they're nurturing their mental and physical health. We all know this is important for parenting.

These parents are showing their children that life is about experiences, relationships and many other things. Most of all, they are exposing their children to a life outside their own home and I think this is a key and necessary aspect of single parenting. They are extending themselves beyond being 'just' a parent; they are being role models for their children because they know their children need to see more than just one side of the story. They still teach their children how to tie their shoelaces, eat at the table and brush their teeth, but it's also about life beyond the front door.

Many women and men make the choice to be a single parent. The women I meet have usually been through surrogacy, adoption or IVF and have spent many years planning and conceiving their child. The men I meet have, in the main, thought a lot about taking their child to soccer and which school they'd like them to go to. None of them lack any love towards their child; in fact, all of them are wonderful parents. However their families are made up is part of the wonderful tapestry of, well, family life!

In terms of a single parent teaching their child, or children, about respect towards others (along with the many other fundamental aspects about relationships), I think it is vital that the single parent recognises that although the way their own family is structured is perfectly acceptable, it is different to the way most families are made up. In other words, the general way of parenting, according to their children, is slightly interrupted by their own unique family. Having said that, there are many, many ways that families are formed – I've mentioned this before – and, of course, it's no-one's place to decide whether any are right or wrong. The important thing to know is when your family is slightly different to most and to recognise the things your children may or may not be learning as a result.

One of my earliest memories is sitting on my living room floor with a Barbie doll in my hand. My father and my grandfather were standing near me, having a conversation about a woman who had been assaulted. It had been in the news and they were talking about how men treat women. I distinctly recall my father saying, 'No man should touch a woman like that and if anyone touched my wife or daughters like that, I know I would have to do something about it.' This was despite my father not being a particularly physical type of person! It resonated with me because I remember thinking that a man had to be strong and protective, not a basher (I think that was the word he used). I know as I've grown up that my father's attitude towards women influenced the type of males I have been drawn to or have connected with.

When you take one of those gender elements away – whether it's a single mum who has never had a relationship with a man or a single dad who has never had a relationship with a woman – or whatever the situation is (and there are many, we know that), how do you teach children about the male and female points of view, because children generally learn by what they see? In terms of attachment theory (and there are vast amounts of research on this), the thinking is that a single parent can be a great one, but you have to do *everything*.

Most of the single parents who I work with are in their mid to late thirties or early forties. Sometimes this has its own set of issues and they are usually around habits. Older parents of young children have had a good few decades of doing what they please, when it pleases them. When it comes to parenting, the easy option is often the most used in regard to things like discipline. This is something single parents need to be mindful of. The secret, as with much of what I espouse in parenting, is firmness, fairness and, above all, consistency. But none of this counts for anything if you aren't prepared to wade in and be mindful of what your child is doing and what's happening around you both, as individuals and as a family.

Intimacy is something that single parents (and let's face it, many parents) may not have much of! This may or may not be an issue on a personal level but it's something that children need to learn and, like most things, this comes from their parent/s. It does not mean you need to go out into the street and treat everyone like a long-lost cousin – that would bring a whole new set of issues – but you do need to show your child that appropriate ways of touching others are okay. You may not be the type of person that kisses people hello and goodbye, but you can greet people warmly by smiling and, if you're not the touchy-feely type, shake hands or go for the neutral zone between the shoulder and elbow and give your friend's upper arm a gentle squeeze when you see them. Teach your child to look at people when talking to them and to use names when they say hello and goodbye. Teach them to be brave and offer help to those that might need it. Doing this teaches them compassion and respect; two things that should come well before physical intimacy anyway. Do it constantly and consistently and they will follow. As they grow older, they will learn on the school bus about sex and all the gory bits, but if you start with the basics, they will be able to put it into perspective . . . hopefully.

Speaking of school, this is a time that things can get a bit tricky for children of single parents. This book isn't about what to do when that happens, but I want to encourage you to get started early in your child's life when it comes to explaining different family types and exposing them to lots of different families and experiences so that *your* child knows that *your family* is normal and okay. Doing this will go a long way towards sending a courageous, confident child to school.

Family dynamics also play a big part in teaching children of single parents. If you're lucky enough to have regular catch-ups with your immediate or extended family, your children will have the opportunity to see how families work. I know a woman whose sister has a family like a spider web – there are stepchildren, exes, exes' parents, exes' exes and the list goes on. When there's an event going on, they're all there and the children don't bat an eyelid. They're used to having everyone around and involved and, provided all the adults behave themselves, they have a great time. The older children in that family know where everyone fits and when the four-year-old welcomed a newborn nephew into the family (yes, you read that correctly), well, their family spider web just got bigger and it's now just a matter of another present under the Christmas tree.

The message I want to give you is that children need to learn that relationships are moving, dynamic, variable and different everywhere they go. Expose them to lots of people, ideas and, most importantly, the workings of lots of different families.

If you're the single parent of a child, you might be wondering how they navigate their early relationships. There isn't really any clear answer to this – in my view, anyway. As their needs change and they grow physically and mentally, there are certainly patterns of behaviour which are influenced by parenting and social norms (now there's another book), as well as their environment, undoubtedly. If your children have a strong sense of place in their home and family and you're giving them a consistent and predictable environment in which to grow, as well as love in spades, have faith, your children will be fine.

Above all, don't lie to your child. It's the worst thing you can do, for both of you. Decide how you are going to tell your child's story to him or her and stick to the truth. You may not tell the whole story all at once but make sure what you do explain is as clear and age-appropriate as you can. You can modify the truth to be age-appropriate but you can never lie. Kids are too smart and they'll never forgive you. You don't have a child as a source of love; you create a human being that is worthy of respect and care with a right to know where he or she came from.

I often think about the changing perception of what's 'normal' and how our children will be affected. The shifts are huge and they seem to be happening all the time but our children still want the same thing. If you are a child and your parent, or parents, miss the little things that are important to you, such as being physically and emotionally present at sports day, for instance, then that's a game changer. Grandparents and carers can fill those gaps but not like a mum or a dad.

My work is essentially with babies and young children but occasionally I see teenagers and we always have the conversation about their childhood. I've seen kids from women's refuges and kids from broken families but they all had a mother figure and a father figure. I've seen kids that have been raised by grandparents with no contact with their parents. The grandparents had taken on the full role as parents. In the last ten to fifteen years, single parenting is now far more widespread and therefore just another part of the fabric of parenting. It may be another ten to fifteen years before we see how these children have managed with a single parent. Now or then, you have to be an incredibly aware person to manage.

Raising a child has to be something that a parent does in collaboration with those around them. The African proverb, 'It takes a village to raise a child', is true. Parents need to provide the safety and security of a loving home life, but they also need to educate and share life with their child, regardless of whether they are parenting with a partner or alone. Your child did not ask to be born. Part of the gig of parenting is to be honest with yourself. Become aware of your failings and admit them. We all have them. If you aren't up for taking a good look at yourself, get someone else to and accept some of the hard things they may tell you. Parenting is about being honest, not only with yourself, but also with your kids.

However you parent your child – single, mum and dad together, two mums, two dads – whatever the combination, you are still a parent. To a child, the strongest example of a human relationship is the one shown by his parents. To a child, the behaviour of adults around each other forms the basis of how relationships work. If parents conflict in front of their children and then openly resolve their differences, the children learn that conflict isn't necessarily something to be feared, rather it's something to work through. If parents show each other respect by listening, talking and caring, the children will learn this too.

Single parenting is simply another type of family. A child's world is shaped by what he sees. If he doesn't see it, he doesn't know it. Single parents need to think about the parenting conversation; the reality of raising a child on their own. It's not about branded cots and prams and where the child goes to school. It's about who the child is and how he fits into his world.

4

THE 'OLDER' PARENT

I MEET a lot of 'older' first-time parents. By this I mean parents having their first baby in their late thirties, early forties or, very occasionally, in their early fifties. There are lots of different reasons for this. Many have wanted to establish a career before they have children and plenty want financial security before having a family. For some, the decision to have children happens later in life. For many parents, it's actually because they've had difficulty falling pregnant. The obvious difference between men and women is that a female's fertility starts to decrease markedly by a certain age and, frankly, if she wants biological children, she just has to get on with it.

I think the most significant thing for older parents is that raising a child is just that much more tiring. It is something I say to an older parent to be aware of. I do believe that people are much fitter and healthier for longer now and this social change allows us physically and mentally to have babies later. But I still stand by my message that when you're older, you tire faster. Parents always need a lot of energy for babies and this need, coupled with levels of anxiety that are probably higher in this group of people – for many reasons – mean that the parenting experience is going to be different from that of a twenty-five-year-old's energy levels and life experience (and expectations).

Let's talk about those expectations, then.

(High) expectations can create real issues. I'm talking about expectations of what the baby will do and how life is going to be with one. This doesn't differ with age, but it's something that needs managing in older parents. On the upside, older parents understand the importance of predictability, stability and the concept of learning patterns in children. They've probably got more patience and understanding to give a child and may be less inclined to think that babies can go anywhere and do anything. Now there are lots of older parents who think that too, but once they do that for a few days and they're feeling tired, they pretty much come back round to the idea of thinking, 'Hang on, we need more rhythm and less chaos in this day'. There's also the very real situation where an older parent has waited years for their baby to come along and they are devoted completely to his every need. So a bit of age can be a great thing!

A growing population of older parents means a growing population of much older grandparents. You can do the maths. A twenty-year-old with sixty-year-old parents means that his grandparents are quite elderly and in fact may have already died. This can change the relationship dynamic in families. When I was little, my grandparents were quite young – perhaps in their fifties or early sixties. But in this generation with older parents, the child's grandparents will be much, much older. They may still be able to enjoy their grandchildren but I'm not sure you'll be able to rely on them to mind the kids for a week while you go on holidays. Even asking a grandparent to pick up your child from soccer on a cold, winter night might be pushing the friendship.

A reality for first-time older parents is that often, they have twins, or more! The reason for this is because as women age, their fertility declines and they might pursue other ways of conceiving, such as IVF. Often, *but not always*, IVF results in a multiples pregnancy. For these parents, this is a whole new level of tiredness and early parenting challenge. There is a lot of community support and this, combined with their life experience, general financial security and patience, means that older first-timers still do as well as their younger, more energetic counterparts. But even if you don't have twins, and even if you're not an older parent, the emotional challenge that comes with parenting is universal. It's this issue that's often the trickiest to deal with.

One of the hardest things you'll ever do for your child is remain 'the adult'. It's one of your jobs as a parent. You need to provide that circle of security, to be 'bigger' than your child, to be wiser and to regulate your emotions in a way that gives him a feeling of being safe and loved. If you can't do it, how can you expect your child to learn and do the same?

This is particularly relevant when parenting toddlers. Unlike toddlers, you are able to regulate your own emotion. For example, you might be watching television and you know the reason you're crying is because you're exhausted and you should get up and go to bed – what's on television isn't really that bad. Your toddler doesn't have that insight so when she's upset, you need to resist getting frantic and complaining about how teary she is or she will think, 'That must be what I am'. It doesn't mean you treat an upset child with disdain, you just need to keep a lid on your emotions sometimes and that can be hard.

Older parents can find this particularly so. Their expectations can run a little skewed and with the combination of fatigue and lack of control (compared to, say, their previous job where they could delegate), emotions can run high. And sometimes, older parents can overthink issues so much that they actually create the next problem. Children really aren't that difficult. They're much more simplistic than we give them credit for. And once parents are able to go back to the basics of what their child actually *needs* – for example, 'Actually, she's crying but she just needs to go to sleep; she's warm, fed, has a clean nappy and she's in a safe, secure environment and now I'm just going to let her have five minutes to calm herself down and see if she can get to sleep herself' – I think the better the whole situation will be.

As for all aspects of parenting, I tend to tell it like it is. I won't gloss over the realities of parenting but I try to present options for parents so they can work things out for themselves. It's a matter of looking at your own situation and making the best of it. Younger parents have loads of energy, but they don't have much life experience. Older parents are a bit further down the track and their expectations tend to be that much greater. There are parents who think, 'Woohoo, let's travel the world with the baby.' In a way they don't do too badly, but these families can be a bit chaotic and while this is probably not a problem for a twenty-five year old, offer this life to a forty-five year old and you'll probably get a resounding 'no thanks'. An older parent gets wearier; they're used to their time and space and they're keen to reclaim a bit of that.

5

GRANDPARENTS

IN my grandparenting classes, grandparents are looking for specific ways of helping rather than the vague notion of 'just being there to do whatever is needed'. The fact that they've turned up to a class (either willingly or not!) means they are there to learn how to *really* help, or someone else wants them to get an update. Either way, grandparents and new parents need to know how to work together so you can all enjoy your new baby.

In most cases, the grandparents in my classes are in their sixties and seventies. All of them are excited about the prospect of having a new, or another grandchild, but they know they won't have as much energy as their parents did when they (these grandparents) had their children. So they're looking for other ways to support *their* children by doing things like some washing or cooking, and they're just as keen to push a pram too. Some grandparents will be taking on the majority of weekday care of their grandchild so it's important for them to know how the reality of this is going to pan out.

I'm always so happy to see grandparents – either in classes or helping a new mum with her baby. There are always a few who, sadly, aren't as interested or want to take over too much or give the new mum a hard time by questioning everything she does. This is a pity because this generally only leads to strained and bitter relationships. I try to encourage grandparents to understand that parenting is quite different now to the way they may have done it. Expectations are different and parents are (usually) older than they were when they had their babies. They aren't completely clueless and, heaven forbid, even dads get involved! It's important to be open-minded and don a thick skin when you're a grandparent. Ride out the first few months wearing your most patient of hats and, trust me, the rewards will come.

If you're about to become a grandparent, I suggest asking yourself a few questions . . .

How much time can you give? If you play golf four afternoons a week, do Meals on Wheels weekly, play mah-jong on Tuesdays and you have thirteen grandchildren, don't offer to drop meals in every night. It won't happen and you'll just be letting everyone down. Offer instead to call in after golf two afternoons a week to take the baby for a walk in the pram, if you've got any energy left! Be mindful also if you have nothing to do but think about the baby and you want to be beside her constantly. Regular, planned help is great – hanging around expecting cups of tea to be given to you while you wait for the baby to wake is not.

How far away do you live? If the distance means staying in the house with the new family, this might be a problem. Maybe it's better to have short visits when you're happy to sit quietly and cuddle the baby and then, when you aren't around, perhaps offer to pay for a cleaner for a few months. For relatives who live overseas, this is a bit trickier. Try to work out sensible come-and-go options that work for you all.

What can you do to help?

Remember that new parents have enough to think about and do without having to prepare activities and job lists for visitors and juggle offers of help. Instead, offer to do specific things, such as picking up older siblings from school or be at the home at regular times so that parents can get out for some fresh air or have a break. Picking up groceries is helpful, as is dropping in a meal or taking away a load of ironing to do.

What's the best way to communicate with new, tired parents?

Try to resist doling out lines like, 'In my day' and 'I wouldn't do it that way' etc. Instead, try saying, 'Where are you at and how can I help you today?' or 'Tell me what's working for you and I'll keep doing that'. You don't need to tiptoe around new parents, just use your common sense and try not to take a grumpy mum too personally!

New mums, I haven't forgotten you either! Most grandparents are very keen to help and the best thing you can do is talk to each other before the baby arrives and figure out what's going to work for everyone. If your parents or in-laws are elderly and really don't have the energy to help run around, give them the job of sitting on the couch holding your baby. Don't underestimate how helpful an extra pair of loving hands can be! They might be the arms you fall into every now and then when *you* need a hug so try to be aware that grandparental help is usually from the heart. Set up a few systems for the first few weeks and be prepared to mix it up a bit if necessary. It's important to eat regularly and well and to get some fresh air every day, so make the most of willing helpers to factor this into your new life.

There are some great resources for grandparents. I like to suggest websites where possible since they are updated more frequently and have links to important information on safe sleeping, car safety and so on. Look in Resources at the back of the book to find a list of websites I recommend.

Tips for grandparents
- Have a whooping cough immunisation every year.
- Do a child-specific first-aid course.
- Understand your son or daughter's style of parenting and ask how you can help.
- Be supportive and try not to criticise.

6

THE DREAM V.
THE REALITY

OST people's dreams of pregnancy and a new baby
are beautiful. The lighting is always soft. Mother
and baby are in warm clothing, all snuggled up and
the dream is perfect. The baby is asleep in the mother's arms.
Everyone is proud and happy. The dream is about bringing the
baby home. The parents have prepared for the baby; bought the
beautiful pram, the cosy cot and the safest car seat. Everyone
is prepared.

Not only is there a dream about bringing the baby home,
but expectant parents have done all the reading. They've accessed
information from so many different areas – their health professionals, websites, books and endless, endless googling. Life is
planned.

Let's go back in time for a minute while I explain why this
can be a problem.

When women were having babies in the 1960s and 1970s, they talked to their best friend and, if they had them, they might have talked to their sisters. They got their information from their close female relatives – usually a mother or aunt. But mostly they worked out motherhood for themselves without very high expectations. Actually, I think mothers in those days might have worked out a lot by simply hanging nappies on the line, which mothers had to do since disposables weren't around then. Pregnant women *noticed* mothers doing domestic chores like hanging out washing. They *saw* the reality of caring for young children. When they stopped work and started cleaning and preparing for their baby, the neighbours were doing the same thing. They started talking and they started learning. Their lives slowed down for the baby.

Statistically, in the 1970s, mothers were working for longer before they had their baby. Prior to the 1970s, pregnant women had somewhere between six weeks and three months off work before they gave birth. In that time, they were able to adjust to a whole different way of going about their daily routine. They saw women outside doing their chores. They were able to see the neighbour's baby chewing on a clothes peg while it was propped in the washing basket. They saw mothers and their families *at home*. The conversations would begin. Expectant mums would see that babies needed time. They could see that their daily routine would change from getting themselves up in the morning, having breakfast, going to work all day, going out for dinner or a movie, coming home and going to bed. And doing it all again the next day. They became aware, *before* the baby came, that their lives would start to shift.

These days, most women work until two or three weeks before the baby is born. In that small window of time, they have Things To Do. They don't see the reality of motherhood in their community. But the dream is still there. They're still going to push the baby in the beautiful pram down the street to meet their friends for coffee. They don't see the mother next door, often because they're doing the same thing. In the week that I'm writing this, I am seeing six mothers in the same street. None of them know each other and they are all experiencing the same issues. If only they knew! If only they knew *each other*!

As a little kid, I knew there was a lady next door who my mother would talk to. I was only three or four but I remember this distinctly. Now I know that in stopping to hang out the nappies and chat to the neighbour, these mothers would be able to pause and think: 'What do I need to do? What does my baby need from me?' They'd be achieving so much more than simply hanging out a load of washing. There was a rhythm to their day which worked for the baby because their lives were generally slower. They may not have had cars so they had to walk to the local shops to get what they needed, mostly on a daily basis. There was time to sit outside and enjoy the warm air while they watched and played with their babies.

Young babies need a slower, more rhythmic life. Whether the baby is sleeping in a pram or a cot doesn't matter as much at this point. What doesn't work is a quick nap in the car while you race to mothers' group before squeezing in a gym class before getting your hair and nails done prior to going out for dinner that night. For a baby, this is chaotic.

In the newborn stage particularly, it can be so easy and so basic. Babies need *time*. And they need patience. And it needs to be rhythmic. The more chaotic and unpredictable your life is, the more reactive your baby will be. If your baby doesn't know or sense what is going to happen next, she will use the only language she knows, and that is to cry. Babies don't have language to say, 'I'm not coping.' Often when I sit down with parents at the newborn stage, they'll say, 'We did a lot yesterday and the baby is crying.' This is your baby's way of saying 'STOP!'.

The sad reality of today's world is that there is nothing or no-one telling parents to slow down. Information is readily available to 'solve' any issues that come up. Parents read that their baby should sleep until seven o'clock in the morning, but the reality is that it rarely happens. If parents are calm and take things quietly, I can almost guarantee the baby will be more settled.

So the dream is there. And the dream *should* be there. Because this is why we have babies!

But the reality is different. And this is when the wheels tend to fall off.

In my antenatal classes, I ask people when they think parenting starts and the answer is often 'When the baby is older'. There is a perception that if you're doing tangible things like toilet training and stopping your child from running across the road, that's when the work starts. But then I mention the early postnatal time in hospital and remind expecting parents that the nursing staff are there to *help*, but *you* are going to look after the baby. About now, I see some very blank, bunny-in-the-headlights expressions.

The distance between the dream and the reality of parenting can be very short if parents are aware of what the reality is *before* they have their baby. And this is what I mean when I talk about slowing down and thinking about what you and your baby are really going to be doing and needing. Post-birth endorphins will get you over the birth and through the hospital stage, but you need to *know* reality is going to happen and the euphoria doesn't last. Having a grasp on the realities of parenting is key to warding off a major crash when the dream fades.

What is the moment when the dream becomes a reality?

The moment when the baby is born can be full of emotion. When you first hold your baby, you can be filled with feelings of love and protection. For some people, this happens instantly, for others, it may be within the first couple of days, and for some, it doesn't happen for a long time. At some point in those first few days, not only are the parents recovering from the delivery, but the overwhelming feelings of 'Well, now we have to feed and care for this baby – all the time' can make those soft-lit dreams fade into the distance and the reality of being a parent come to the fore!

Going back to when your parents were looking after you, your mother would have stayed in hospital for seven to ten days where she was nursed back to health. Her baby went to the nursery between feeds and at night. She was physically feeling well when she left hospital. Today, we have parents that are leaving hospital any time between four hours and five days after giving birth. In Sydney, the average length of a mother's stay in hospital is around three days. Mum goes home feeling a bit physically wrung out, she has a tiny baby and she goes into a community where the message is: 'You can do this.'

I love the custom of some Asian communities where the mother goes home and has a 'sitting in' period of about forty-two days from when her baby is born. She is nurtured by and learns to care for her baby through the guidance of her mother, aunts, grandmother and perhaps her sisters. She fully recovers and she does well. On the other hand, I see women who 'have to be down the street to do something' three days after the baby is born, and some who are isolated by distance from family and friends.

The only place you need to be, three days after your baby is born, is at home, in your pyjamas, with your little baby, preferably with someone handing you something to eat and drink. You need to be feeding and cuddling your baby. You need to get to know your baby. Allow yourself to play with your baby's little hands and fingers. Feel how wafer-like her nails are and how soft the soles of her feet are. This is *really, really* important.

7

PREPARING FOR YOUR BABY

So, you're pregnant! Congratulations! Now to get ready . . .

You don't need to spend a lot of money preparing for the arrival of your baby. Allow me to repeat that:

You don't need to spend a lot of money preparing for the arrival of your baby!

Having a baby is a very exciting time and, like most parents, you will want 'the best' for yours. This is admirable, but babies don't know the difference between a $5 singlet and a $50 one. What matters is that you have the right size and your baby is dressed appropriately.

If it's the first of your intended three children, you will need to spend your money wisely on a few items:

- Car safety (capsules and car seats)
- Sleeping (starting with a cot is fine, but a bassinette is a

cosier environment for a small baby)
- Mobility (a pram).

Research these carefully. Work out what you can fit into your budget as well as your house and car. *And stick to that budget.* I think you can get very good items from major chain stores. All baby products sold in Australia have to meet Australian Standards safety requirements. The Australian Standards sticker should be prominently displayed on the item. If you can't see it, don't buy it.

Babies grow very quickly. You don't need everything in all the colours of the rainbow. If friends offer hand-me-downs, accept graciously.

Clothing and nappies

Here's a list of what you actually need:
- At least two boxes of newborn nappies – if you're wondering about the girl/boy difference, the boy nappies have a little more padding in the front
- A dozen cloth nappies – trust me, these will come in handy
- 6–8 singlets – winter with sleeves, summer without
- 6–8 long-sleeved, long-legged bodysuits for winter; short-sleeved, short-legged for summer
- Baby socks, and winter or summer hat
- Warm top or jacket for winter.

You need clothing that is easy for you to take on and off your baby, comfortable for him and easy for you to wash and dry. Forget the leather pants and crystal-studded t-shirts. They'll do your head in. Hang them decoratively on the baby's bedroom wall instead.

It's important that newborn babies' clothes fit them properly. If you buy them too big, they aren't snug enough to keep your baby warm. If you need to get an idea of what size to buy, mention this to your doctor and they'll be able to tell you if you're going to have an 'average' sized baby, or otherwise. 'Average' is about size 000 at birth. Buy clothing in cotton, wool or bamboo, not polyester.

Baby wraps

Babies should be wrapped up until about twelve weeks. You will need:

- 6–8 light muslin or cotton wraps for summer, and jersey or slightly thicker material for winter.

There are lots of different versions of wraps, such as nifty little suits with velcro fastenings, but I think wrapping with squares of material gives the baby a better feeling of security. It's important to settle your baby's body for sleep but, as she gets bigger and older and she can self-settle a lot more efficiently, the body-shaped wraps will be fine. They are quick and easy to use – particularly if you don't have much practice!

Sleeping bags are for when your baby is rolling around so you won't need them for your newborn. When your baby starts moving around more, she will bust out of her wrap and even though she may not wake up, she will get cold – that's where the sleeping bags come in handy. This usually happens somewhere around four to five months.

Bedding

Babies sleep better in smaller environments. If you can borrow a bassinette, do so. If you borrow a bassinette (or a cot), make sure you buy a new mattress for it. Your baby needs:

- A cot or bassinette and a well-fitting, new mattress – your baby does not need a pillow
- Three sets of linen (again, cotton or bamboo is best)
- A light blanket for summer, a heavier one (light wool) for winter
- A couple of light blankets for the pram.

Make up the bassinette or cot following the SIDS guidelines at www.sidsandkids.org. This site is updated regularly so make sure you check in frequently to ensure you're up to speed with the latest research.

Changing nappies

When you are, or anyone else is, changing your baby's nappy, here's the most important thing you all need to know:

NEVER LEAVE YOUR BABY UNATTENDED ON A
CHANGE TABLE.

Babies do fall off change tables so prevent this by keeping one hand on your baby *at all times.*

You'll be changing nappies frequently for a couple of years, so make sure you set yourself up so that you won't compromise your back:

- There are standard change tables you can buy, but the top of a chest of drawers will serve you well

- A change mat that's padded for comfort, and a cover for the top to alleviate that warm-bottom-on-a-cold-plastic-mat feeling – a towel will do the trick nicely
- Baby wipes – you can buy them (hypo-allergenic ones) or use water and soft disposable cloths (or reusable ones if you're up for the washing).
- Nappy cream – use a zinc-based barrier cream; there are plenty on the market
- A bin for the nappies – nappy bins are debatable – your regular household rubbish is fine, just make sure you pop the really soiled ones in a disposable bag first. If you have twins or more, you may need to order an extra garbage bin from your local council. Seriously, there are a lot of nappies.

A quick word on disposable things: We each have our views on the environment but I say, at this point, do whatever makes your life as easy as possible. If you're concerned about reducing environmental pressure, you can always drive less and walk more, hang washing on the line instead of putting it in the drier, etc – you'll work it out.

Feeding

Although it's not absolutely necessary and room size might prevent it, a chair in the baby's room for night feeds would be good. You might like to use a feeding pillow for comfort in the early weeks. For general newborn feeding, you will need:

- A breast pump if you're expressing (or want to)
- 6–8 bottles (fewer if you're breastfeeding)

- Slow flow teats (these will change as your baby grows)
- Steriliser
- Bottle brush
- Basic baby formula
- Bibs (sometimes putting a bib on a newborn is an academic exercise – they're just way too big – use a little soft cloth or the corner of a muslin wrap instead).

Bathing

The basic requirements for bathing newborns include:

- A couple of towels – not necessarily bought for the baby, but the baby's towels need to be kept separate from the rest of the family
- A couple of face washers
- A simple baby bath
- Baby bath solution – I tend to start with oil-based products
- Baby moisturiser – the simpler and purer, the better
- Nail files – they're better for tiny babies than nail scissors or clippers.

Going out

Good car safety is essential. You need to make sure you buy the best quality car seat you can afford. You also have to make sure it suits your situation. If you need to carry the baby in the car seat for any distance, such as from a car park or garage to your home, it should be light, easy to install and remove from the car, while remaining comfortable for your baby. After all, there will be times when your baby is asleep in the car and you'll want to carry her to the house while she's in the baby seat – without waking her up!

You can rent baby capsules which will accommodate your baby up to about nine months. These are useful as they're light and easy to get in and out of the car. You can also buy reversible car seats that will accommodate your baby from birth until she is about four years old. After that, you'll need to buy a booster seat. See Resources for the Australian National Child Restraint Laws website.

There is a limit to the amount of time your baby should be in the car seat. This is not a great environment for your baby to be in for any length of time. If you're going on a long car trip, stop regularly to give everyone a stretch. Similarly, if your car seat clicks into a pram base, be mindful of the amount of time your baby is in there. It's easy to drive somewhere, switch the seat to the pram base and, before you know it, a couple of hours have passed since your baby has had a good stretch out.

There is no law to say that your car seat needs to be installed by a registered child-restraint technician. However, if you are struggling to work it out, you should get help. Look online for your nearest fitter. Once the seat is in and fixed, ask them to watch you take it out and refit it. It's worth it, trust me. See Resources for some suggestions.

Pram

Your pram needs to be of sound quality and it needs to be safe. These are the two main criteria. In Australia, it is against the law for a retailer to sell a pram without a red brake step and a wrist-strap.

Apart from that, you should consider manoeuvrability. It may be that you have two prams – one for walking and one for whipping out of the car when you're at the shops. Think about where you live, what you like doing and get something that suits you. As your baby grows, you may change your pram again. Don't be lured into thinking what works for everyone else must work for you. In other words, resist the temptation to follow trends with things like prams. You really need to think about your own body and your situation and purchase something that suits. One of the most popular prams on the market today is very narrow and lacks the leg depth needed for a child beyond eighteen to twenty-four months old. Make sure you can lift, carry, set up and fold down your pram easily and it fits in the boot of your car.

Sun protection is very important. You need to be able to keep the sun off your baby, without restricting air flow. The darker the colour, the warmer the pram will be. I see so many people pushing prams that have a thick cover over the top of the pram, usually tied onto the handle or pegged down. There isn't an inch of space where air can get in. This is *not* okay. Without air flow, it can be significantly warmer inside the pram, especially on a summer day, and this of course means that you could overheat your baby.

Even if the sun canopy is large, make sure there is ventilation towards the back of the pram. Think of yourself sitting inside a tent on a hot day. You've only got the front flap open for air flow – it would be pretty stuffy in there, wouldn't it? Now imagine shutting the front flap as well and think how hot it would be. Good air circulation is essential for your baby.

Baby bag

There'll be times when you feel like you're carrying your own bodyweight in baby paraphernalia every time you leave the house. Everyone has different needs but I suggest that some essentials should always be in your baby bag:

- 4 nappies
- Some disposable nappy bags
- A cloth nappy
- Wipes
- Sample-sized creams
- Sample-sized hand disinfectant
- A small change mat
- Any feeding equipment
- An extra wrap if you're breastfeeding
- Space for your things such as your wallet and phone
- A spare change of clothes for your baby.

Unless you're travelling, you're probably never going to be too far from home or a supermarket, so resist packing everything you own. Remember to replace things as you use them so you aren't caught short next time you're out.

8

LOOKING AFTER YOURSELF

I F you're a good passenger on a flight and you listen carefully to the safety briefing, you'll know to put on your own oxygen mask before fitting your child's, right? This is a great analogy for parents. I could use all the usual sayings like 'It's a marathon, not a sprint' and so on – but the fact is, parenting is a long-term gig and unless you consistently take care of yourself, it can be harder than it ever needs to be. By taking care of yourself, I mean making sure you eat and sleep well, exercise and have fun (that's keeping physically and mentally happy!), share the load with others and accept offers of help when they're forthcoming. The last bit is particularly necessary with newborns.

In my antenatal classes, most people say they expect to get *help* from family and friends, and *information* from their health professionals and the internet. There are a couple of things I need to point out here. Friends are usually in the same boat – that is, they have a child or children of their own to care for – or if they aren't, they generally have very little idea of what you are going through. As for family, yes, they love you and don't want to see you having a hard time, but the reality is, your parents may live a long way away, or they might work, or they might simply prefer to play golf! Siblings with their own families will try their best to help you, but like friends with families, they're flat out too.

Working out how your family and friends can help you requires a bit of thought on your part. You need to work out what you are going to *need* in the first three weeks. As a mother who may be breastfeeding, you are going to need a lot of food for the energy you require to get through these early few weeks. You're also going to need a lot of *time* for yourself (to rest) and for your baby. Think about eight feeds a day in the newborn period and each feed taking about an hour. When you include the feed itself, changing nappies, cuddling and snuggling, that's eight hours of your day taken out just sitting down. And then you have to define 'day' – because in newborn parenting world, a day is twenty-four hours, not just daylight hours. A baby doesn't think in daylight and dark hours.

When you understand this, it will help you move from the dream to the reality of parenting. For the first fifty or so days of their lives, babies are meant to feed and sleep. They have to take in a lot of fluid to enable their bodies to grow. They have short periods of sleep so they have the energy to feed again. Forget about routine for now. Even if family and friends keep asking you about your baby's routine, just remind them that life is around-the-clock for now.

But back to looking after yourself. You will get tired. Not the tiredness of a late night out that an afternoon nap will sort out. It's like jet lag; a sort of fog that you can walk through but you can't get out of. Except jet lag goes away. But if you know that your body is changing and you allow the physical and mental changes to come and go, and you allow yourself to accept that you will be tired and that there will be changes in your day-to-day life, you will cope a lot better.

Some notes on changes in your relationship with your partner – remember, you're both in la-la land at the early birth stages because often, if it's dad going back to work, he probably hasn't returned to his day job yet. He's still as much in dream world as mum is. He's probably still wondering if the car seat is in properly or how to manoeuvre the pram through the checkout at the supermarket. Or maybe he's checking the mailbox twice a day for the mini-Liverpool Football Club strip he ordered weeks ago. (Who cares if the baby's a girl?) Dads need to be looked after as well because, unlike mums, they don't have the surge of hormones that will sustain them through weeks of broken sleep and breastfeeding. Women have a physiological (as well as emotional) reaction to having a baby: hormone levels fluctuate and endorphins and oxytocin are released during birth; prolactin is released for breastfeeding. Men tend to get overwhelmed with emotion in a completely different way. Suddenly they feel entirely responsible for keeping it together. They are concerned about their partner – they've just seen her go through something very physical and, although they (hopefully) were clued up about what to expect, it was nothing like what really happened. There are difficult labours, difficult deliveries, sick babies and, even when the baby arrives screaming loudly but looking beautiful with a perfectly round head, dads are still hit with the reality of: 'Oh my God – this baby is real and now I have to care for it!'

Think back to how life was when your father became a parent. Mum had the baby in the hospital and Dad looked into the window of the nursery and saw a washed, wrapped and usually sleeping baby. His emotions were probably more in check. He probably felt a bit overwhelmed when he brought your mother and you home, but he quickly went back to work and that was it, really. Parental leave was non-existent; he may have had a week off but this was unusual. His role was clearly defined as the breadwinner and your mother would have done all the parenting. Today, many might think this is outrageous but, in those days, your mother would have known this was what was expected of her and she accepted that she was going to be at home caring for the baby. She noticed the neighbour hanging out those nappies and she knew another new mum down the street. Remember I mentioned the saying 'It takes a village to raise a child'? It's true, except that village is now a lot smaller and things, I think, are a little tougher.

Family and friends, meanwhile, still want to help you but you have to understand that you can't rely on them to do everything. Family support might be sporadic due to distance. Friends are working and have their own families. You may not have parents or friends around at all. Your family, the older members in particular, may not have experienced the same feelings you will. By this I mean that, despite perhaps living in a city or having neighbours that don't live too far from you if you're in a regional area, you may feel isolated. This is because, again, mothers these days are programmed to believe they can do it all by themselves. They don't tend to reach out to their friends and family for help, or even seek company on a bad day.

But you have to. Because if you're supported and calm, your baby will respond in the same way.

In the first few weeks, this is the time when you are most likely to get the most offers of help. Use it wisely! There may well be the expectation that you can get up in the morning, have a shower, clean the house and make your mother or mother-in-law a cup of tea before breakfast. Know that expectation is there, but ignore it. If you've got any lying around, treat yourself to a clean pair of pyjamas and snuggle up with your baby on the couch. Long-term, you will both benefit.

You need time. You will need to adjust your daily rhythm so that you can slow down and get used to a quieter, slower life (for a while, at least). Ignore talk of 'you can do it all' and 'back in my day'. Think about what *you and your baby* need and put in place ways that others can help you.

Taking care of yourself in a physical sense is important too. Buy food that's easy to prepare and healthy for you both. Meals needn't be complicated and leftovers are perfectly fine. If you're heading out for some fresh air with the baby in the pram, pick up a few veggies or some salad. Do a weekly shop for protein – meat, fish, chicken or a vegetarian option. Add the veg or salad and you've got yourself a meal. Let the oven do the work. Keeping the necessities simple is key. If you're on a budget and a gym membership is not going to happen, walk instead. As long as you're eating well and moving every day, you are doing beautifully!

Postnatal depression is serious and something you need to be aware of. If you think you are just 'not feeling better' after your delivery, or you are struggling to get through the day, teary most of the time, or you feel overwhelmed, talk to your doctor. Partners can suffer, too. Remember that help is available, treatment is effective and recovery is possible.

9

PREMATURE BABIES

Let's first define what a premature baby is. A baby born between thirty-seven and forty-two weeks gestation is called a 'term' or 'full term' baby. A baby born at less than thirty-seven weeks gestation is then, of course, defined as a premature baby. In America, premature babies are known as 'pre-term'. In Australia, we often call them 'premmies' – it's just a colloquialism; they are the same thing.

There is also what is known as 'extreme prems' and these are babies that are born from twenty-three weeks to about thirty weeks gestation. In the last two decades, medical care for these babies has improved extensively and thankfully many more have a higher chance of survival.

If a baby is born at thirty-two weeks gestation and has no particular medical circumstances causing early labour (in other words, mum just has a premature labour), delivery is safe and everyone is well, this baby has a really good chance of survival. Often, premature babies struggle to feed well as their suck instinct is yet to develop. When they're in hospital, staff tend to put them in the 'feed and fatten' group! Usually, premature babies need some assistance with tube feeding to make sure they are getting the nutrients they need.

Lung development is also an issue with premature babies. Mothers who are looking like they are going to have a premature labour, where possible, are injected with a hormone to aid maturity to the baby's lungs. This is beneficial in changing the condition of babies when they're born.

The biggest risk to a premature baby is infection and this continues for a while even after they are at home. Premature babies are fragile, even though they may have done well within their prematurity. I always reinforce to parents that their prem baby is still very little, she still has difficulties and everyone needs to be careful. Just because premature babies look strong and robust doesn't always *mean* they are strong and robust. You need to use your common sense and be firm about staying away from sick people, avoiding crowded areas in the early months and generally being aware of your baby's needs.

Usually, the first concern that parents have is how well their premature baby is doing. Obviously the earlier the baby is in prematurity, the longer they will need to stay in hospital. Those little babies can still have lots of early issues, but what I generally see in the community is that they often do very well in their development – they just catch up at different rates. When I see a cohort of premature babies at age one, they're still doing really well for either their adjusted age or their actual age. Some will have caught up to their actual age and they're reaching all their milestones for a one-year-old, and some are doing really well at their adjusted age, which is minus their prematurity.

From my experience with premature babies, the issues they have over the long-term are those really subtle things, such as being slow to read. My nephew was a thirty-five weeker and he had gross motor problems, but they were addressed in the early years and now he's fine. Even though premature babies may not be diagnosed medically with an 'issue', or they don't miss really big milestones, sometimes I just see these tiny little things. Granted, prematurity may well not be the cause of the 'issues' I come across and, with assistance, preschool milestones are often met with ease. With prems, I'm just aware that they might lag a little and I remind parents that they might need a little bit of assistance. Awareness and acceptance are my messages here.

Be mindful that correcting or adjusting age for premature babies is a bit of a moving beast, so to speak. Not all parts of a child mature at the same time – and this goes for children who were not born prematurely as well! Maturity is going to shift and change all the time. I tell parents that they have to look at the (very) big picture and resist relying on the chronological age or the corrected age of their child. You might get two babies, identical in age, let's say six months, with one lying on the floor, playing under a play gym, being wrapped up and snuggled down to bed. The other might be exhibiting behaviour closer to a six-month-old, rolling around, holding her head up well and slightly supporting herself in a seated position with the ability to stay awake a little longer. Be flexible and remember that your baby is unique.

So your baby is premature – now what?

Parents going home with a premature baby (or babies) always wonder how to care for and *live* with their baby! It's a month by month thing, I think. As I mentioned earlier, raising a premature baby is about working out actual age versus adjusted age, being flexible about those parameters and then seeing where the baby fits within that window. There is a lot of support for parents of premature babies and parents should seek it out. I have this theory about getting premature babies safely through their first winter. If parents can get their prem baby through her first winter without getting a major cold or a chest infection, they've done really, really well. This can be hard if your premature baby has siblings, especially if one is an active member of the infamous toddler germ pool. But if it's your first baby, you can mimic what the hospital has taught you in terms of hygiene and, really, common sense and care should get you through.

Don't be afraid of your premature baby. You won't break her. Most parents are involved from the moment their babies are born – you're no longer looking at your baby through a glass window while she sleeps in the corner (okay, so the excitable toddler cousins might, bless 'em!), it's all hands on deck these days. Parents are allowed to touch their babies – in fact, it is encouraged. If a premature baby is stable and simply nurtured to grow, she can be moved with minimal risk. Nowadays, there's more contact and parents have more knowledge; they're involved in the process from the first day, and all of these things empower them to feel that they can get through these early weeks and months. Of course, parents are told the risks along the way and they're informed about everything. So there's less secrecy and fear and, even though it's an incredibly difficult time for them, they're stronger for the knowledge and often feel more confident when it's time to go home.

Regular assessment is part of having a premature baby. For example, if you thought there was a delay in speech development, you should probably get on top of it quicker, rather than saying, 'Well, that might mature in six months time'. In the right circumstances, and in the right way, it doesn't hurt to give premature babies a little bit of extra stimulation at age-appropriate times. In my view, it's important for parents to address these things before they (potentially) impact the child later in life. Establish consistent assessment with someone, whether it's your early childhood centre, your paediatrician or your GP – just make sure it's the same person so that subtleties can be monitored.

Premature babies and feeding

Premature babies are very good mixed feeders. That means your prem baby is likely to enjoy feeding from the breast and the bottle. As a newborn, your baby may have been tube fed but as she has grown, so has her ability to suck. In hospital, the staff would be doing a thing called 'grading feeds'. This means your baby might have one feed today of the sucking feed, whether it's a breast or a bottle, and then she will have a rest, because for a prem baby, sucking is tiring! In a couple of days she might have two sucking feeds, and then a couple of days later she may have three. Between these sucking feeds, your prem baby will be tube fed.

By the time you are all ready to go home, your premature baby will be feeding well. You can choose whether you are going to fully breastfeed, or whether you continue to breast- and bottle-feed. There is always pressure on parents to do one particular type of feeding but, really, these babies actually prove that you can do mixed feeding quite successfully and still make great progress.

I think the hardest thing for parents of prem babies is that they're caring for a little baby for a long time. Unlike parents of a full-term baby, who feeds around-the-clock for six weeks and then the gaps at night start to get longer, the prem baby might be in that around-the-clock stage for three or four months before parents start to see that gap getting bigger. Parents often say to me that they feel like they don't get out of that 'really *young* baby' stage for a long time. For instance, parents of a thirty-four weeker could have twelve weeks before seeing some sort of lengthening of a sleep pattern.

It is important for parents of prem babies to understand that their baby is probably not going to extend his night feeds until he's at a corrected age of being able to do that. When I hear from parents of prem babies, it's around the time they want to know when their baby is coming out of that stage. So each of those little steps just takes longer for prems to do but, generally speaking, if the feed is graded and we can see the baby develop, their feeding is okay. Feeding problems might include a sucking or attachment issue which is worth discussing with a lactation consultant. A good lactation consultant will be able to check for other issues such as tongue tie. If feeding issues are addressed properly, the baby will do fine; it's just a slow process and understanding this is key.

I always tell parents of prem babies that their baby is unique and to resist comparing her with other babies – even other premature babies – and certainly not to their first, second or third baby. All children are unique, but with prems, there's just a bit more sitting, listening and looking that needs to be done!

There is a lot of support out there for parents of prem babies. Most major hospitals have a support program in place and after the unique friendship they've formed while sitting in NICUs and special care units for a long time, parents get to know each other well. It's like a little posse of friends with whom they can share the highs and lows. It's a unique passage of time for them.

Premature babies and sleep

Prem babies are very tired when they're born. Often, nursing staff will do feeds while they're asleep and keep handling to a minimum because this just takes up energy. They get a little cuddle and then they're put back down. This pattern is something that parents quickly adapt to and one that they take home. They learn that overhandling a prem baby creates fatigue and a tired baby takes longer to progress. It's a quick lesson and something they've been putting into practice for sometimes many, many weeks.

The biggest shock to parents of a prem baby is coming home with a baby that has slept a lot in hospital but starts to change as she matures. Their well and active baby is starting to become more alert and with this alertness, sleep is often not as deep up to the point of the next feed because the baby is maturing – she is shifting and changing.

At some point, your premature baby's game of catch-up will run its course. One day you might be watching your baby and it will occur to you that she has been doing something very similar to her playmate that was born at full term. It's exciting and a time of huge joy to see your little one doing well. Good on you, too!

10

ADOPTION, SURROGACY, FOSTERING

WHEN I see people who are about to meet their surrogate, adopted or foster baby, I'm always amazed by their resilience and their stories. Some have been trying to have a baby for many years. Many have had several miscarriages, some have had babies that have died. Some have medical reasons why they can't have children. There are males who have had a vasectomy and women who have had tubal ligation – some by choice, others not. I have met people who have been in accidents and their fertility has been affected. Then there are the people that we hear about in the media – superstars who are 'too posh to push' and others that 'buy' their babies. Whatever they're doing and whoever they are, the desire to have a child is just that: a desire to have a child. There is a long history of loving parents out there, whether they're same-sex couples, whether they're a mum and dad who have never conceived, whether they're single people who just want to be parents – they all want to start a family and surrogacy, adopting and/or fostering has been an option for them.

I believe parenting a surrogate, adopted or foster child is a mindset. Parents of these babies are still *parents* – it's the journey prior to birth that is different, as is the story they're going to tell their child, but I'll get to that later.

People can be extremely opinionated about surrogacy, adoption and fostering but, in the end, it's about creating a family. In my work, I am seeing more adopted and foster babies going into families from birth and the adjustment is the same as for parents of a surrogate baby. When I meet the parents-to-be of these babies, it's usually when, for surrogates, the surrogate mother is around twenty-six to thirty weeks gestation, and for parents of adopted and foster babies, their baby is ready. The realisation that 'We're really going to be parents!' has dawned upon them. They can see themselves with their baby or babies (often there are twins), and they contact me to see what they need and when, and to learn what to expect. I love hearing from them and it's always a time of great joy and anticipation. Regardless of how their family is made up, it's business as usual and we work together to settle baby and parents into a family life together.

The arrival of your baby

The birth of a surrogate child is an emotional time. When the baby is born, she is handed to her surrogate parents straight away. They go to the nursery or to the room where they're staying and their new family life begins. A lot of these couples say to me, 'I thought I'd just feel love', and can be disappointed or confused if this doesn't happen. I always advise that love is a feeling that grows and I don't think many people fall in love with their babies until a period of time has passed. For others, it may be instant; perhaps when they are lying there quietly and looking at their baby. They get a feeling which some might *call* love but I think it might be more like protection. Some couples worry that the surrogate mother will want to take the baby back and they won't feel better until the documents are signed and they have the birth certificate that says they're the parents of the baby. It's a real and understandable feeling.

Surrogate parents, in my experience, always show great respect for the surrogate mother. They make sure there is a lot of support throughout and after the pregnancy. It's not like the surrogate mother has the baby and goes home and puts on a load of laundry. They have usually been sourced through an agency and, as far as I have been aware, they are well compensated and cared for.

Parents of adopted and foster babies can have a different experience as they may only have, literally, a moment's notice that their baby is ready. They may have been waiting for years to hold their baby and they are understandably overwhelmed by what is ahead of them.

In terms of the day-to-day development of a surrogate, adopted or foster baby, there is no difference between them and a naturally conceived child. I don't separate them into a group and, in fact, most of the time I simply forget about how the baby arrived and just focus on helping the family.

Telling your child's story

The psychology of these families is something I'm often asked about. I'm not a psychologist but I don't think you need to be one to understand that children want to know where they fit in the scheme of things. Children love hearing about their birth and the story of how they got to be part of their family. It forms a perception of how they see themselves. We know that even children who have been adopted into beautiful, loving, secure homes and have wonderful lives can still struggle with the fact that they're adopted. Children want to know where they come from and where they belong.

Parents that I've worked with have approached this in different ways. A lot will approach it with the story that there was a birth mother and she carried the baby for the parents as a very special favour. Children of parents who tell this story know their true story from an early age. When they are a bit older, they learn that there are different ways to make up a family but with support and truth, they get used to their story pretty quickly. They might ask a lot of questions later on, but the story remains the same, it's just the detail that fills it out and gives it context.

If children are not told the truth (obviously in an age-appropriate way), this can lead to a trickier conversation as they get older. Don't underestimate a child's ability to be disappointed with parents who have not told them the truth. If they're unsure, or they've been lied to or there's deception, or they're not really being spoken to, then they start to wonder why: why didn't you tell me? Why couldn't you tell me that? Why don't I have a mother? Why don't I have a father?

My advice is to keep the story simple and truthful. The earlier they hear the story, the better they accept it. When your baby becomes a toddler, a whole new world of curiosity opens up. The questions are endless and often quite confronting. When a toddler asks, 'Where did I come from?', he's looking for a reasonably credible answer. He will know you're avoiding the question if you tell him, 'You popped up in Dad's beer', or that the stork dropped him in. Agree on a truthful version of your story and stick with it.

11

TWINS AND MORE

AUNTED? Excited? Both? If you're having twins, it is quite normal to feel overwhelmed at times. You're probably wondering how you're going to cope so let me assure you of this: you'll have double the work but double the delight.

I meet a lot of parents of 'multiples' either before they have the babies or in the early weeks of bringing them home. Most want to know what they need to set up for multiple babies and what to expect in the early weeks. What I try to do is provide an idea of what to expect and what works. For some, twins will be their first babies, and for others it can be their second, third or sometimes fourth pregnancies! In every case, each family has its own unique set of circumstances.

A multiples pregnancy can bring its own set of anxieties so I generally meet the parents at around thirty weeks. This is so we can set up a nursery by around thirty-five weeks in case of an early delivery. Multiples are usually born before full term and women pregnant with twins or more don't usually feel like running around getting things ready in their later stages so, all in all, it's a good idea to get organised.

Preparing for the arrival of multiples

BEDDING

At some point you will need two cots, but this isn't necessary at birth as twins will fit in one cot for a period of time. At this stage, you're better off borrowing a couple of bassinettes as they will be smaller. Your little babies will sleep better in a cosier environment. Remember, they've been curled up inside you for nearly nine months so they are used to being snug. The usual bedding of natural fibres is best and make sure you have plenty of wraps.

CAR SEATS

If you have other children besides your multiples, sorry, but you may need a new car. Consider the practical aspects such as the age of your older children and the ease of getting everyone in and out. You will also need to be able to move the babies from the house to the car without too much fuss so this will influence the type of car seats that you get. There are great car-seat hire companies that can help with configuration. See Resources for some suggestions.

PRAM/S

The very first thing you need to consider is whether your pram will fit in your car. I see lots of people heading back to the shop with a pram for this very reason. You need to be able to lift it as well, so choose carefully. You may end up using two prams in three years, or two different types of prams – one for walks and one for the shops. Consider ease of function such as getting through doorways. Many prams have an option to use car capsules within the frames. Lots to think about, I know, so take your time to weigh up your options.

CLOTHING

Remember that a lot of people will give you clothing so don't go overboard buying outfits for your multiple babies. They will grow quickly so my suggestion is to have 6–8 each of singlets, bodysuits, wraps and socks and, depending on the season, whatever extra warmth you might need. That really is plenty to start with. It's also important to make sure you have clothing that fits as babies stay warmer in the right size.

SENSIBLE THINGS THAT WORK
- Two good quality baby rocker seats
- A feeding pillow for either breast- or bottle-fed babies
- A couple of bottles for newborns with slow flow teats and possibly a small electric pump in case you need or want to express
- Often, twins will use dummies to help with settling – have a few on hand in case.

Development

In terms of their development, your twins or multiples are the most amazing creatures to watch. You will put the same energy into each of them and, regardless of whether they are identical or fraternal, two very different children with two very different temperaments will grow. As you watch them develop in the first twelve to eighteen months, you will notice that they might 'leap frog' each other. One baby may roll and the other may take another month to do so. But that baby may be the first to sit on her own. Have patience with them and enjoy watching them grow.

Feeding

The idea of feeding twins (or more) can be overwhelming. The main thing to remember is that when feeding twins you need to feed them at the same time or within the same time frame. If they get out of sync, you could find yourself feeding numerous times over the day/night period.

There are many feeding combinations for twins so make sure you get some good advice. You can fully breastfeed, fully bottlefeed or if your babies are having trouble with feeding you might be breastfeeding with bottle top-ups as well. Feeding takes up a lot of time so it is important that you are all comfortable. Breast- and bottle-feeding pillows are available for twins which can be a great help – but a word about twin bottlefeeding pillows: twins are often less than 3 kilograms each at birth and because they are so small, it is important they are well supported when feeding. It can take four to six weeks until they are bigger and stronger enough to be more stable while feeding so, again, get some good advice to ensure you are giving your babies every opportunity for a comfortable, efficient feed.

I am often asked if parents should wake a baby to feed with the other and, generally, the answer is yes. When the first baby wakes, you should gently wake the other so she is alert for her feed. If you don't, you could take two hours to feed if you have a really sleepy baby. In the early days I suggest feeding one baby and then waking the other straight after so that they feed in the same window of time.

Sleep and settling

Once your babies have been fed, it's time for sleep. As I mentioned earlier, most twins will sleep together for a period of time before they sleep in separate cots and even then, they will sleep in the same room. They get used to each other's sounds and they almost become each other's white noise! Most parents will struggle at some point with sleep and you may need to separate twins for a short period but ultimately they can sleep together. Just like all babies, twins will need to learn to sleep in the same way that I have written about throughout the book. Interestingly, I find that twins settle better than single babies. As you are settling one baby, the other may start to settle by the mere fact that you can only do one at a time. Sometimes life is like that!

Getting help

It is a *very* good idea to get some extra help if you are expecting twins, or more, especially if you have older children. People will be eager to help so let them, but be organised as to how this will work best. The biggest help you can get is going to be with meals and washing, as well as hands to help with feeds and changing. The most chaotic period of the day, particularly as your babies get older, is in the afternoon to evening, say from about 2 pm until 7–8 pm. If you have older children, this is when they want your time as well. Help with the babies allows you to have time with the older children.

Parenting multiples

I work a lot with parents of multiples, whether the babies are their first pregnancy or their fourth, and I think my main piece of advice is this:

Don't get too far ahead of yourself. Think in really short periods of time.

When I'm working with families, I often speak about getting through only the next couple of weeks at a time and how important it is to have people around you that are working *with* you. Whether you rely on your community or mothers' group or a trusted professional to get some advice, make sure you can speak up about things if their advice is not working for your babies or your family as a whole.

12

BABIES WITH SPECIAL NEEDS

THERE'S a reason why the word 'spectrum' often comes up in conversations about kids with special needs. It's because the range of 'need' is huge and it varies with every new medical discovery or test. There is also an increasing level of awareness about special needs within the community and, happily, a growing number of ways to help kids with special needs have long and fulfilling lives.

When a baby is born with an obvious special need, health professionals tend to diagnose early, either during pregnancy or at birth. The baby might be premature, or have a genetic makeup that requires special needs, or have physical deformities that require special care. There are babies who are born presenting as normal, healthy babies and along the way, usually in the first two years, don't develop in the same time patterns as other children. It can be anything from speech issues to low muscle tone, and it may not be picked up until they get to a stage of cognitive development, usually in toddlerhood. In most cases, being way beyond or below the average milestone markers is a reason for concern.

Parents usually know when something's wrong. I'm a huge believer in gut instinct (don't tell the scientists!) so if a parent raises a concern, I listen carefully. A child's parent has to be his strongest advocate; you're the one who should go out to bat for your child, and no matter how mild you think the issue is, you have to persist until you get the answers you need. You need a trusted ally who will allow you to say, 'Actually, I think there's something wrong with this baby,' so persisting until you find a GP who is willing to listen and understand you is important.

Once a diagnosis is made (if there is one), you need to accept the support provided within the community and embrace the life you are going to live. Your child needs you, just like every other child needs his parents. Accept that there is a period of adjustment to work out what is happening and what you will need to do.

Finding out you have a child with special needs

I remember sitting down with a couple and their newborn. They had no idea that their daughter was going to be born with Down syndrome. They just kept looking at her in the cot, with no emotion. Her mother kept saying to me, 'How are we going to cope with this little girl, what are we going to do?' And I said to her, 'Well, there are two things that you need to do. One is you need to grieve for the child that you thought you were going to have; the dreams of the life that you thought this child was going to bring to you. The second thing you need to do is embrace the child you've got.' It was a delicate and difficult conversation.

I do believe that once parents are able to do those two things, the child really develops in a very healthy and loving environment. It's okay to grieve the child you thought you were going to have, and it's important that you accept you have a child that is going to need much more from you than you ever expected. Then you have to love them. And that love will come as long as you accept what's in front of you. When you talk about your child, use her name, not her need. Don't say, 'This is our Down syndrome baby, Christine.' Instead, say, 'This is our daughter, Christine, she has Down syndrome.'

And you will adore her.

13

SICKNESS AND YOUR NEWBORN

NEW parents often fret unnecessarily about their baby getting sick. That said, you do need to be careful, especially in the period before your baby is immunised and if you have other children. At this stage, it's more about prevention than cure.

In these very early days and up to about six weeks, your baby is very vulnerable, health wise. He has protection from breast milk (if he is breastfed) but is still at high risk. I wouldn't suggest taking your baby out regularly to, say, big shopping centres. I would definitely go out where fresh air is circulating around him but I'd be more wary of crowded environments.

Older siblings can be right little germ carriers! School and preschool aged children are in an environment that often carries airborne viruses. While they have some immunity, their newborn sibling does not. When children are between the ages of two and, say, six or seven, they aren't very hygiene-aware and often play lots of hugging games with buckets of snot being wiped on sleeves and hair pets leaping from one head to the other (need I continue?). They often race home from day care or school and head straight for the newborn for a lovely big warm cuddle. The nits will be annoying but the colds and viruses always present more of an issue.

My tip to parents of newborns with other children is to give them their bath when they get home from day care or school. Get the dirty clothes off, pop the kids in the bath and they can put their pyjamas on, or in summer, some shorts and a t-shirt. Some parents are reluctant to do this for fear of breaking up routines for the child or children. It's worth it for the baby's sake and the kids will get used to it. Simple. Treat it as a growing and learning exercise for the older siblings. Teach them that their new brother or sister can get sick easily and this is how we look after him or her. Antibacterial gels are also easy to use so don't hesitate to whip them out if the hordes arrive and they all want to cuddle and squeeze the newborn.

When little babies get sick, they can get *really* sick. They can go downhill quite quickly. Although the most they will catch is a head cold or a chest infection, this can be really uncomfortable for a young baby so you still need to be aware of your surroundings. It's difficult for parents who are dropping kids at day care and school because they're among the odd snotty nose or cough, so stay aware and wash your hands regularly.

Another good way of keeping your baby protected is to use the pram or pouch when you're out. By keeping your baby as covered as you can, you can always divert sticky hands and super-friendly 'hellos' by saying that your baby is 'having a little rest now but would love to say hello later'.

Once babies get bigger and stronger and their immunisations kick in, they are able to assimilate into environments with a lower chance of getting sick.

Practical ways of dealing with sickness

My book isn't about the diagnosis and treatment of childhood illnesses. Fantastic resources are out there so I'll leave you to seek those out. The main thing is that if you think you should see a doctor for your child, you're probably right.

If your baby is under six weeks old and is unwell, she will be pale and listless. She'll be lethargic. Feeds will be pretty short and she may be very sleepy throughout the feed.

- The first thing you should check is your baby's temperature (which *in a baby without an elevated temperature* should be in the range of 36.5 to 37.5 degrees Celsius). If it's 36.5 degrees, your baby is okay. If it's 37.5 degrees, I'd suggest taking her temperature twenty minutes later to check.
- If your baby has a blocked nose and watery eyes, she may be getting the start of a chest or head cold.
- The next thing you need to do is to give your baby energy. You will need to feed her. Even though the feeds may be shorter, you need to maintain her fluid intake.
- You also need to make sure your baby can breathe properly through her nose. This is important – she needs to be able to suck to feed and she won't be able to do so if she can't breathe through her nose. Use some gentle saline drops which are available over the counter from your pharmacy.

Chris's What If? cupboard

Every home needs a basic first-aid kit. We know this. My What If? cupboard has things in it that I'll never need unless it's two o'clock in the morning:

- One or two feeding bottles
- Breast pump
- Dummy, or two
- Digital thermometer (an ear thermometer works better after 6–8 weeks when your baby's ear canal is a little larger)
- Infant ibuprofen
- Infant paracetamol
- Phone numbers for your GP, pharmacy, poisons information
- A ready reckoner for first aid and infant CPR.

An important note: You might be wondering why I've got a breast pump and bottles in there. If you've got a listless baby who is struggling to feed, you can quickly express some milk, pop it into a bottle and give your baby a feed without her using the extra energy she needs to feed at the breast. *Now is not the time to engage in a bottle versus breast argument.* Your baby needs fluids to help her get better.

So now you're feeding your baby frequently and keeping an eye on her temperature. If it rises from 37.5 degrees Celsius, you need to cool the baby down. Perhaps remove some of her clothing and run a tepid bath. Don't make her cold – shivering increases the body's temperature. After the bath, take her temperature again. If it's lowering, you're doing well. If it's rising, it's time for action. If it's the middle of the night, head for the hospital. Just on that one – make sure you know that private hospitals do not have an Accident & Emergency unit. Know where your nearest A&E hospital is. If not, call an ambulance on 000. If it's during the day and you know your GP's surgery is open, give them a call.

Time for a little aside here: *Before* your baby is born, find a good family medical practice that has after-hours support. Write down the phone number and stick it on the fridge. In fact, find out about all the health providers in your area, including the local pharmacy. Write down those numbers as well and put them somewhere handy. Most babies do not get sick between 9 am and 5 pm. That would be far too convenient.

First aid – when things are life threatening

There are times when you need to act very quickly. You'll know when this happens. Cuts and bruises need action too, but you can offer sympathy at the same time. When it comes to choking and falls, you need to be on the case. I always encourage parents in my antenatal classes to do a first-aid course, one that includes baby CPR. There are many out there, just make sure you get one where you can ask lots of questions. See Resources for suggestions.

14

BREAST OR BOTTLE?

I THINK there are so many pressures on parents these days. I truly believe that parents come from a place of wanting to do the very best they can for their children. For me, that's the most important thing. This applies to feeding your baby. My job isn't about advocating any particular way to feed your child – it's about helping you to decide what is going to work for you and your family and then supporting you to do it.

The first thing that parents need is knowledge. Your first attempt at breastfeeding is not likely to be the beautiful, romantic notion of sitting in a lovely white dressing gown while your baby feeds off the breast. It is a learned experience and like millions before you, you will encounter the occasional difficult stage. For some women, the baby attaches beautifully on the breast with no problem at all; for others, there is real difficulty in getting the baby to feed well. There is a multitude of reasons why that happens but there are wonderful lactation consultants who can help you to breastfeed successfully. If you're worried or you have particular issues that you think will create problems with breastfeeding, make an appointment to see one before you have your baby.

Breastfeeding is not always as easy as you perceive it to be. When you hear people talking about feeding their baby, there's an expectation that they're talking about breastfeeding. But for some mums who have struggled to breastfeed, it can be hard to speak honestly about their experience and their choice to bottle feed. Others have no problem talking about how ever they fed their babies and I applaud this. It's each parent's choice.

Some women are pushed into breastfeeding when they actually have never wanted to. For whatever reason, some mothers simply do not want to or they don't find it enjoyable, but they do it because they think they have to. My sister didn't breastfeed and she has two perfectly beautiful, normal children. They never had a drop of breastmilk. They don't have allergies, a second head didn't grow out a back shoulder; nothing happened to them. They are perfectly normal.

Likewise, if you want to breastfeed your baby, you need as much support as possible. Whatever you do, I encourage you to think about your whole family and how you can best manage.

Regardless of how a mother wants to feed her baby, her decision needs the support of her partner, family and health professionals. For a first child, a mother can put all her time and effort into establishing breastfeeding. She can work at it harder and can get a lot of advice. For a second-time mum or a mum of twins or multiples, this might be much more difficult to do because she's pulled in a lot of different directions. So at some point she will stand back and make the decision about what is best for her family. As a community, we need to support busy mothers with really good information.

For a mother returning to work, giving up breastfeeding need not be necessary. She's put all that time and effort into establishing breastfeeding and then feels like she has to give it up because she's going back to work three days a week. Mums like this need to be able to say, 'I want to continue breast-feeding, how do I do it?' Our job as professionals is to give her the best advice possible so that she can make an informed decision about what is best for her and her baby. She might think, 'Okay, well now I know what I need to do to maintain a supply of milk, I need to think about getting the baby on a bottle and who's going to care for her while I'm at work. I need to find out where I can express milk at work, and how I store it and get it back home again.' These are big issues to think about but they are most certainly not insurmountable.

Many mothers I know breastfeed for a few months and then wean, for a number of reasons. Again, a mum needs support to wean and then manage a new way of feeding her baby. The advice I give mothers is to work out what they can manage and go from there. If that means a breastfeed first thing in the morning and last thing at night, and formula in between, then that's what I support a mum to establish.

Feeding is one part of caring for a child; it's not all that you will do for your child. I don't believe there should even be an argument for or against breastfeeding or bottlefeeding. I know that this really disturbs some people but, in my view, parents need to do the very best they can with what they have and be supported in a way that helps them and their family.

15

WEANING

WEANING comes in two forms. You can wean from breastfeeding to bottlefeeding or you can wean from milk feeds to solid feeds. It's difficult to identify a specific time and way to wean because every mother and child situation is different. Weaning can also be baby-led.

Whether that's self-weaning from breastfeeding to bottles, or whether it's self-weaning from milk feeds to solids, at some point a baby will take the initiative. Your baby might be pushing and pulling back and screaming as you try to put him on the breast. If you sought help and things aren't improving, I would suggest your baby is saying, 'This isn't working for me'. There is a point where I think you have to be respectful to the baby and you need to say, 'Actually, this isn't working for us', for whatever the reason. This is a form of weaning.

There are some mother–baby relationships where they mutually wean. The baby might be much older and far more interested in food. He may not need as many milk feeds so it just mutually happens between them. These babies often breastfeed past the age of one and the more independent the baby becomes, the fewer breastfeeds he needs.

There is also abrupt weaning where, quite literally, your baby takes one feed and then refuses others. It could be a scenario where the baby simply says, 'That's it, I'm not going to do it anymore.' Or it could also be on a medical basis where, whatever the circumstances might be, it means a mother has to abruptly wean her baby.

The most favourable scenario, obviously, is the mutual one. If you know you're going back to work at nine months, then from six months you might start to wean your baby onto bottles. You'd need to wean your baby onto a bottle since, at this stage, he is too young to get the quantity he needs from a cup. A good lactation consultant would be able to give you a plan to follow so you can happily and gently wean your baby. A good lactation consultant would also recognise if breastfeeding is not working for you, and be able to help you make a plan to move on to the best way of feeding your baby.

Weaning can be very emotional. I tell mums who are doing a gradual wean and coming to the last feeds that it's okay to feel sad and it's okay to feel guilty, but you've got to move on because there's another guilt round the corner with children! Remember those quiet times in the middle of the night when you were feeding your baby? Do you recall when he started sleeping through the night and, despite the fatigue, you felt a little twinge of sadness that those quiet nights with the two of you were gone? And now, notice how much your little baby has grown into the child he has become. That's progress. Congratulations, you've done a great job.

16

SOLIDS

I TEND to think babies are developmentally ready for solids – which is any food that isn't milk – when they reach around five months old. Fundamentally, this means they are able to hold food in their mouths without tongue thrust; that is, resisting anything in their mouths that isn't a nipple or a teat. If you put a food-laden spoon into the mouth of a baby with tongue thrust, he will just push it out.

The problem, however, is that there are no defined regulations about when, where or why to start a baby on solid food. Health guidelines change and, of course, since each baby is an individual, it really needs to be up to you to be aware of your own child, his needs and above all, to take things slowly.

In my experience, I come across two distinct reasons why parents want to start feeding their child solids before the child is ready. The first is because they think that starting solids will help their baby sleep through the night. In other words, a full tummy equals a sleepy baby. The reality is that health professionals don't say that food and sleep are related unless a baby is particularly underweight.

The second is that parents are ready to do something different with their child. A tiny bit of boredom has set in and they are keen to see their baby develop. Often, there is a suggestion from someone in their mothers' group to start solids or they think that because all the other babies are starting, theirs should too.

To be fair, there is a very mixed message in the community about solids. Parents seem to be looking for reasons to start or solutions to problems when, really, looking towards their child for cues is the best way to know when to begin.

When to start solids

One of the first and most obvious reasons to start solids is when your baby seems a lot hungrier. She will seem unsatisfied after coming off the breast or at the end of a bottle. She will be looking for more food, perhaps waking up earlier for feeds and sucking her hands more vigorously. She actually looks like she is looking for food! Another sign that a lot of people use is when, at about four or five months, your baby starts to watch you eating food with a bit more interest (other than simply looking at something that's moving).

The third, and probably the most important factor, is to look at where your baby is in terms of age and development. If your baby is only four months old and you feel she should start solids, then you need to begin slowly and with very small meals. At five months, some babies are still simply not interested; but then at six months, they are quickly taking two to three meals a day because, developmentally, they're ready.

It is a tricky thing to navigate. I usually suggest starting solids at around five months, when your baby is taking all of her milk feeds and, developmentally, she can hold her head still so that she can actually concentrate on eating. You don't need to put your baby straight into a high chair – in fact, high chairs are quite hard for a baby to sit straight in until they're about six months old. You're better off to start in the bouncy chair where your baby is sitting straight but leaning back a little.

There's another school of thought called 'baby-led weaning' and this is where babies are rarely spoonfed meals; they just use their development to pick food up and put it in their mouths. I don't necessarily disagree with this, but I think it's better introduced at an age when babies can actually do this. This is usually around six to seven months old. I do think you need to offer foods for your baby to hold, even if you are spoonfeeding. A mixture of the two is better so your baby gets to feel what food is like as well as tasting it. It can all get pretty messy but, remember, your baby is exploring tastes and textures.

Parental attitudes to feeding

Parents usually fall into two categories when it comes to feeding their children. There are the sharers who offer pieces of the family food, such as peeled cucumber cut into sticks from the salad and bread from the loaf in the middle of the table. There is a lot of finger food and often bits and pieces of age-appropriate family food is passed to the baby while the rest of the family eats. There are also parents who worry a lot about choking so they puree everything and spoonfeed for a long time.

There are issues with both. The first group needs to make sure their child eats well at meal times, particularly if there is a preference for one type of food. The second group needs to make sure their child's eating habits develop appropriately. It is quite rare for a child to choke on a large piece of food, instead using her gag reflex to get it out of her mouth. Remember, children use their tongues to move food around in their mouths and they use their jaws and teeth (if they have them) to chew food. At around seven to nine months, your child will be able to effectively do this in a way that will break the food down to a manageable size to swallow.

Obviously you need to keep an eye on your child while she is eating and know what to do if she does choke (see Resources for first-aid courses). Sitting down to eat is teaching your child good manners as well as ensuring she is safe.

The first feeds

I often suggest to parents they try a first feed of solids at around four o'clock in the afternoon. At this time, your baby will have had an afternoon sleep and is likely to wake hungry. Several years ago, it was the thing to give a baby their milk feed and then offer solids, but I disagree with this method. If your baby is full of milk, he is unlikely to try solid food. If you offer a small meal before the feed, your baby will still take the majority of the milk feed afterwards. If you overfill your baby with solids and he doesn't get his milk feed, he will probably wake up at night for the rest of the milk feed.

I'm often asked whether I think breastfed babies take to solids better than bottlefed babies. I don't think it makes a difference at all. There are some babies with feeding issues, such as difficulty coordinating the jaw and tongue movement, and there are children with very low appetites. Sometimes speech therapists and nutritionists need to be consulted but the majority of kids are okay. If you start solids at the right time and you're predictable and you have an understanding of what your baby needs, he will go on to eat really well for the first eighteen months. At this point, his appetite tends to ease off into what I call 'the hibernation period'; this occurs when your baby decides, 'I only need to eat what I want when I want it', but that's a bigger discussion in the chapter, Toddlers.

Positioning your baby so he can eat well is important. Babies don't sit particularly well in high chairs when they are only five months old so a bouncy chair works better. It's on enough of a recline for your child to hold himself still, so you're going to have a better chance at connecting the spoon with his mouth! Make sure you're at eye level with your child because if you stand over him, he will have to tilt his head back to look at you.

You will need a small soft spoon because your baby has a little, soft mouth. Make sure the food you offer is appropriate, warm and the consistency of a puree. I suggest it is the consistency of thickened cream. It should flow, but there's a definite thickness to it.

I tend to start babies on rice cereal. It's one of the foods that is pretty safe in terms of allergy. People tell me all the time that their babies don't like it, but I maintain it usually has something to do with texture and warmth. If you make it properly, there's a fair chance your baby will eat it. Lots of parents tell me that their babies get constipated on rice cereal but, remember, for nearly five months, your baby has only had fluid in his system so when you start feeding him anything that is thicker than milk, it's going to take a little while for him to move it through his body. If it's too thick, it will be stodgy and gluggy in the baby as well.

For the first meal, make up one teaspoon of rice cereal mixed with breast milk or formula. Mix it to the thickened cream consistency. I always offer water with a meal for extra fluid. It's a good habit to get into. With every two to four days, gently increase the amount of rice cereal you give your baby, depending on how he is coping with it.

Meal development

For the first week to ten days, just feed your child one thing (the rice cereal mixture). Because it's only a tiny amount, you're not reducing fluid intake. If you mix up the meals too early, such as giving your baby carrot one day, pear the next, then potato, avocado and so on, it will be too much for her to cope with. Instead, after a few days increase the *amount*. One little heaped teaspoon of rice cereal mixed with liquid probably equates to about ten teaspoons of food for a baby. Don't forget, in the short term, you should be giving your baby a milk feed after solids. Three to four days later, increase the meal size and then, three to four days later, increase it again. At about two weeks, add in a little bit of flavour, such as a small amount of pureed fruit. A word of caution here: your baby will probably love it but you need to resist pureeing fruit endlessly and feeding simply this. Pureed apples and pears are lovely but they have a lot of sugar and obviously this isn't the ideal food to continually (and only) be feeding your child.

Developmentally, the pureed foods will continue to about seven months. Somewhere between six and seven months, if your baby is interested, she will start to eat some form of finger food in her own way. By seven to eight months, the baby is looking for more texture and goes from a sucking response off a spoon, which is puree, to a chewing response. So the texture of the food needs to come up to the consistency of a mash. From about nine months, you will move fairly quickly to offering foods the consistency of risotto.

Mouth physiology

Your child will learn to use the bones (and eventually teeth) in her jaw, a chewing action and saliva to break down food in her mouth and her tongue to move food around her mouth. I know lots of babies who don't have a tooth in their head until they are twelve months old but could eat a small lamb cutlet.

The early physiology in your child's mouth needs to change from a sucking action to a chewing action. This means the tongue has to move differently. By offering lots of finger foods, you are helping this change to happen – it's pretty noisy while the sucking is going on but she'll get the hang of it! This change in mouth physiology continues to develop further until her tongue is so efficient, it will be used for talking.

Meal sizes and expectations

Regardless of the age your baby is when she starts solids, portion sizes need to start small and gradually increase. Resist the temptation to feed your baby until she stops eating.

The message you need to give your child is that meals are predictable, that you will feed her, and that eating needs to be regulated; that is, you don't eat everything on the table. As adults we realise this so it's up to you to teach this to your child. As your child grows up, she will learn that eating is about choosing how much and what to eat according to taste and appetite.

In the early days, a teaspoon of rice cereal is enough when you're mixing it with breast milk or formula. It looks tiny, but it's enough. Knowing how much to give your child is an important part of the rhythmic pattern of introducing solids. This is because developing the pattern of having healthy, varied food at regular meal times goes a long way towards helping your child understand different food components. She will try different textures such as purees when she starts solids, mashed food by the time she is about seven and a half to eight months old, and then food the consistency of risotto by the time she is nine to ten months old. Throughout this development, your child will develop a window of independence where she will want to feed herself. You'll see her grabbing food, squeezing it and perhaps using language to talk about feeding herself such as 'me do it', 'I do it' and 'myself'.

You need to be aware of how much is enough. Once babies get the idea of eating, they often bang the tray top while you're getting a meal ready. This is their way of saying, 'I need food now', 'I like it, give it to me!' When you get to this stage, you can be confident that your baby understands that it is food time: we sit down, we are going to drink water, and she will be given enough food to eat.

Age-appropriate foods

Once your baby reaches about nine months and she is enjoying food the consistency of risotto, barring any food allergies, she will be able to eat the same food as the rest of the family. Getting out and about is so much easier because you can cut up most food to suit your child. Kids this age are also pretty good at regulating how much food they want to eat so things like pasta, soft vegetables, risottos, toast with toppings such as avocado – even pizza crusts – are all easy, great foods.

Social reform and food

Eating is a social behaviour and this can be no more apparent than at preschool or day care. This is particularly so if parents are working and it's tricky to sit down together for regular meals during the week. Children tend to eat better at day care, because that's where their little friends are sitting around all eating lunch and snacks together. There are kids that will use their hands to eat and there are little ones that still need to be fed, but they're all watching each other and generally having a great time.

Easy menus

Parents often unfairly judge themselves on how much and what food they feed their children. There's really no need. Yes, I do think parents need to take responsibility for the health of their children, but not at the expense of their sanity!

If you are time poor, resist the urge to feed your children with food out of a packet, especially the ones that you give your child to suck on – you know the ones I mean. I'm all for a bit of convenience and I know there are times when packets of food are incredibly handy – travelling, for instance – but all it takes is a bit of planning and a trip to the supermarket, and it isn't difficult to provide small, healthy meals for your child. Cook in bulk, freeze portions and remember you can all eat the same foods, only some members might need smaller portions that are chopped up. Frozen vegetables are fine, pasta is great and don't forget the good old egg in its many forms.

There are some fabulous cookbooks on the market with easy recipes and ideas for kids' food. See Resources for a few suggestions.

Food games and getting the balance right

As a parent, all you need to be concerned with is if the meal you are giving your child is reasonable. Is it fresh, healthy, developmentally appropriate and reasonably portioned? If you answer 'yes' to all these, then it is a reasonable expectation for your child to eat it, or at least try it.

It takes a number of days of not eating before you die of starvation, so missing one meal is not going to hurt your child. It will, however, give him a very strong message that you are not a short-order chef. Parents sometimes say to me, 'But he'll go to bed hungry.' It's up to you, obviously, but if your child goes to bed at seven o'clock and doesn't eat for twelve hours, he will be fine. He might just eat all his breakfast.

The more food games you play, the more you set up your child for a lifetime of that behaviour. You do need to make sure that you are giving your child the chance to eat well and learn about food and meal times. Don't leave it too late to feed her dinner. I think it is reasonable to feed children between 5 and 6 pm. This obviously changes as they grow, but for young babies and small children, this is a good time for dinner. At around 5–5.30 pm, blood sugars do drop, which is one of the reasons you see tantrums in that window. Make sure dinner is ready and they are seated and eating at around that time and they (and you) will be able to cope with the end of the day much better. Turn off the television, take any electronics away and sit down with them to talk.

Timing and number of meals vary with different cultures. Some cultures feed their children every couple of hours, others graze all day. Some feed three meals a day, others have a larger hot meal in the middle of the day and a small supper in the evening. Generally speaking, if you want to feed your child between meals and you want them to eat three main meals a day, you need to make snacks very small and light. Half a banana or a few blueberries is ample. Again, being realistic about what you're feeding your child will go a long way towards happy meal times.

Our modern world is so busy but even though our mums might have fed us the same meal every night because there wasn't as much variety at the supermarket, we were fed *meals*. We sat down together and we talked. Meals were about family time and, for me, this is the key to getting kids to eat well. It's about conversation and sharing together. Set your children up for this and these early, happy days around the table will be memories they will have for life.

CHEAT SHEET:
SOLIDS

THE BASICS . . .

Always make sure meals are warm as they will be easier to digest.

Pureed fruit is pretty much sugar with a bit of fibre so resist making it a meal on its own. However, if your baby is constipated, a meal of pureed pear should get things moving – but only do this once and then go back to the 'proper' meal.

Fruit puree should be used to add a little flavour, not replace a whole meal.

Increase the amount of food served slowly, so that the bowel can get used to solid food.

SUGGESTIONS FOR YOUR BABY'S FIRST MEALS

FIRST DAY AND THEN DAILY FOR 2–3 DAYS

- If bottlefeeding, make up 90 ml of milk

- 1 teaspoon rice cereal + warm milk (mix to a creamy consistency)

- Offer the remainder of bottle or 1 side breastfeed

2–3 DAYS LATER

- 2 teaspoons rice cereal mixed with warm milk

- Offer the remainder of bottle or 1 side breastfeed

2–3 DAYS LATER

- 3 teaspoons rice cereal mixed with warm milk

- Offer the remainder of bottle or 1 side breastfeed

2–3 DAYS LATER

- 3 teaspoons rice cereal mixed with warm milk

- Add 1 teaspoon pureed apple or pear for flavour

- Offer water after meal in a sippy cup. This may take some time but soon they will manage the cup.

2–3 DAYS LATER

- 3 teaspoons rice cereal mixed with warm milk

- Add 2 teaspoons pureed apple or pear for flavour

- Offer water in a sippy cup

Hold your baby on this amount for a week or two. At this point you could start offering your baby a second meal during the day.

THINGS TO NOTE . . .

Don't increase meal sizes until your baby is taking the whole amount for 2–3 days. This can vary, so don't worry if it takes a week!

If your baby is not ready for solids (i.e. there is a lot of turning away, spitting and refusal), stop and start again in a week.

Increase meal sizes by a teaspoon for 2–3 days at a time until your baby can finish 3 teaspoons of the rice cereal/milk mixture in a meal.

Once your baby is happily eating 3 teaspoons of the rice cereal/milk mixture, you can add a teaspoon of pureed pear or apple to the meal, or mixed it in with the rice cereal/milk mixture.

Offer water in a sippy cup.

17

SLEEP AND SETTLING

S LEEP is a huge topic of conversation and concern for parents. It can make or break families and it is one of the main reasons parents call me for help.

For parents of newborns, one of the first things you need to know with regard to sleep is that you can't spoil the baby in terms of how you sleep them. You just need to keep things very basic. When your baby needs to go to sleep, wrapping becomes the signal, slowing his body movement down so that he can quieten his body and go to sleep. How your baby actually goes to sleep in the first six weeks doesn't really matter. You can cuddle or rock – whatever works for you and your baby. What matters is that he has a consistent pattern of going to sleep and that he has the chance to be *able* to sleep. Sleep is very important for your newborn since it provides the energy to feed. Without it, your baby will be too overtired and sleepy to finish feeds, will then have short sleeps because hunger has woken him or the overtiredness will make him struggle to settle, and so begins a vicious cycle that takes a lot of work to break.

The second factor in helping your baby to sleep is their environment. If your baby is in a nice, quiet area, he is more likely to fall asleep. There's a myth out there that babies will sleep anywhere and everywhere. That's probably true for the first ten days of a baby's life where they go into quite a deep sleep, but it's not true long-term.

The importance of wrapping

Many people tell me that their baby doesn't like to be wrapped and they try different swaddles that are more loosely wrapped, without success. If you choose not to wrap your baby, try looking at yourself in a mirror as you hold your baby. Notice how your baby tucks into you with his arms close to his chest as he calms and drops off to sleep. When you go to lay him down, he likely startles and wakes up. Wrapping is important in helping your baby to quieten his body; to help him settle and sleep longer at this young age.

Settling your newborn

Once your baby has had a good feed, a clean nappy on, a warm cuddle and you feel he is ready for a sleep, wrap him and hold him until he is calm, then put him into his bed. It may take a few minutes until you know he is relaxed enough to go off to sleep. Settling your baby is a matter of learning what he responds to best. Some babies go off to sleep quickly, then wake a short time later; others take more time to settle off to sleep. However it works for you and your baby, take this early time as a learning process. You might have to pat, rewrap, stroke, gently rock or pick up your baby. Give yourselves time to see what works; get to know what your baby likes and what he responds to. At this age, there are no bad habits.

Bedtime rhythms

The idea behind creating bedtime rhythms is that you are helping your baby to learn a sleep pattern. The basics of any rhythm is that you need to be consistent and you need to keep things simple.

So, for instance, if you rock your baby to the sound of the Beatles for the first twelve weeks of his life, every time he comes out of a sleep phase you need to crank up the Beatles and rock him to sleep again. When your baby is twelve weeks old and nice and heavy, it will be very difficult to say, 'Actually, I don't like this anymore and I'd like you to get yourself to sleep independently without me and without the Beatles.'

However, if you concentrate on your baby getting a good feed, you wrap and cuddle him and then you provide him with a quiet environment in which to sleep, you're going to have far greater long-term success. Feeding is important. Getting to know the baby is really important. Wrapping helps to give your baby an indication that he will be going to sleep and the environment should be quiet.

Family life is also about visiting people and going places. If you remember the basics of a good feed, wrapping, cuddling and a quiet place to sleep, you should be able to do this quite happily. If you have a place you regularly visit, set up a spot that's perfect for those visiting sleeps. I'm sure most grandparents would love to help you with this. It could be in the bassinette of your pram, providing it's safe. We know babies can handle change, but they can only handle a little bit of change in small amounts. Of course, some babies are great sleepers and some are not so good – just remain consistent with yours and if things don't work out, try not to worry too much. Perhaps grandma can visit you at your place until the baby gets a little bit older.

Growing up

As your baby becomes more alert during his awake times, especially around six weeks and he can move his head and look around, I think it's important to add an extra step which involves learning your baby's cues to go to sleep. You need to start gaining an understanding of your baby's awake and sleep time frames. Common signs of tiredness include little arm and leg jerking movements, whingeing and generally looking uncomfortable and frustrated. This is in addition to the obvious signs such as yawning and rubbing his eyes.

Most of this is simply getting to know your baby's cues and this takes time because he's always changing. If you look at the different age chapters, you will be able to see a rough guide as to what your baby's sleep needs are as he grows.

Again, sleep is important because it's when babies grow. The good thing about having a pattern of some description is that it gives you something to focus on in an effort to regulate your baby's day when things get chaotic.

My main message about sleep is that if you put the work in from a young age and you're consistent, your baby will actually develop a very good sleeping habit regardless of the 'routine' that works for you as a family.

What your baby needs

I'd like to praise all parents out there who say, 'I'm going home to put the baby to bed.' Why? Because sometimes it takes a bit of courage to leave a function, or a gathering (like mothers' groups), to take your baby home to his regular sleep spot. Not only is it important that your baby sleeps, but if you're clued into things, you can find a little bit of time-out for yourself as well.

There's a lot of pressure on parents these days and when you have someone chirping in your ear about the way you parent your child, you need to be strong and calm. Focusing on what your baby needs, particularly in the first twelve months, is key to long-term sleep and settling success. The essence of this book is about what your baby *needs* and how you can nurture those needs and enjoy parenting.

If you look at parenting over the years, and certainly in many other cultures, family plays a huge part in raising a child. There always seems to be someone willing to cuddle the baby. In many cultures, the baby is not taken out at all for the first six weeks. I think the first year of your baby's life should be about his needs, not yours. In a short space of time, you'll get longer spaces where your baby's awake and you'll be able to go out a lot more, but in the early weeks and months, you should keep things consistent and this means staying close to home. It doesn't mean your baby needs to be in his bed every single sleep, but he needs the consistent settling patterns and environment to be able to sleep regularly and well.

SIDS

One of the biggest fears new parents face is the fear of SIDS (sudden infant death syndrome). This is also known as SUDC (sudden unexpected death in childhood). It is most important that you keep up-to-date with current information and take care of your baby according to the SIDS and Kids guidelines (check them regularly at www.sidsandkids.org). In short, they recommend sleeping your baby on her back, placing her to the bottom of the bed, maintaining a smoke-free environment, having a firm mattress and bed for your baby, and tucking your baby in.

If the whole concept of sleep was as simple as this, I think it would be very clear what parents need to do, but there are so many other factors that come into it and things can get really confusing. What if you have a baby who flips over at a really young age? What if you have a baby who starts moving around at four months? Babies as young as this can move backwards, roll to their side, roll to their front; they may roll in one direction but not back again. Many parents are filled with anxiety because they have these guidelines that are going to keep their baby safe, but what happens if they've got a wriggler?

The guidelines, however, are very clear for a newborn so make sure you follow them closely.

18

ROUTINES, RHYTHMS AND CHEAT SHEETS

I AM always asked about routines. Generally speaking, I tell parents that a routine can only exist when a baby wakes at a familiar time every day; however, parents can use a rhythm to understand their baby.

Throughout this book, I have encouraged you to think about what your baby needs before you set about buying things, changing your day or, indeed, changing your baby's! My suggestions for *routines* will be much easier to implement if you are aware of your baby's *rhythms*. Every baby is different, as is every family. What works for one may not work for the other. If you're unsure about where to start, my Cheat Sheets are a good place to begin. They often work for my clients and they are easily adapted to meet a family's changing needs. This often includes other children, going back to work, day care, Great Aunty Jo's 90th birthday party or a trip overseas.

For me, this is all part of parenting but, again, if you can understand what your baby needs, the rest is pretty straightforward.

A bit of fine print . . .

All routines and rhythms in this book are general in nature. They should form the basis of a broad pattern for families. Most babies will start their day between six and seven o'clock in the morning and that is the time when parents need to pick up their baby's cues to feed and sleep for the rest of the day. Rhythms and routines need to be fluid and flexible. The reason my Cheat Sheets are in this book is so that if your baby is all over the place, they are a starting point to give order where there may be chaos!

As your confidence grows, you and your baby will develop your own patterns that work for you. This will happen if it's your first baby that you're all getting to know, or it's a fourth baby fitting into a busy family.

19

YOUR BABY – BIRTH TO TODDLERHOOD

WELCOME to the first years of your baby's life! Since babies have general stages at which their sleep and feed patterns start to change, each stage has its own Cheat Sheet. All babies are different so these figures are a *guide* as to what yours will generally need. You may need to tweak the times to suit your individual baby. It is important to learn to read your own baby's unique way of saying, 'I am tired and it's time for me to sleep.' Be guided by her tired signs, which for babies up to four months may include grizzling, frowning, jerky movements and clenched fists. For babies from about five months, tired signs might include grizzling, yawning, eye rubbing and ear pulling. Most babies have one unsettled period each day. This is often from one feed until the next and is most common in the evening. On average, babies under six months of age will have one unsettled day each week. If your baby is under six months and wakes after less than one to one and a half hours of sleep, you should attempt to resettle her.

Age	Rhythms	Total daily sleep time	Awake time between sleeps	Length of sleep cycles	Play
1–4 weeks	Feed, sleep	16 hours in 24 hours	45 mins–1 hr	2–3 hrs	Talking, faces, singing, cuddling
4–12 weeks	Feed, play, sleep	15 hours in 24 hours, 3–4 day sleeps	1–1.5 hrs	1.5–2 hrs day sleep, lengthening night sleep	Toy frames, mobiles, soft toys, colours, floor play, tummy time
3–4 months	Feed, play, sleep	8–10 hours per night (includes night feed/s), 2–3 day sleeps	1–1.5 hrs	1.5–2 hrs day sleep	Bats at toys, holds small rattles, books, music, moves body more
4–6 months	Feed, play, sleep	8–10 hours per night (possible night feed/s), 2–3 day sleeps	1–1.5 to 2 hrs	1.5 hrs	Holds, touches and mouths toys. Transfers toys from hand to hand.
6–8 months	Feed, play, sleep	11–12 hours per night, 2 day sleeps	2.5–3 hrs	1–1.5 hrs	Transfers toys from hand to hand, mouths toys, toys with moving parts, rolling, working on sitting

Age	Rhythms	Total daily sleep time	Awake time between sleeps	Length of sleep cycles	Play
8–10 months	Wakes at a similar time in morning and in a similar pattern at night	12 hours per night, 2 day sleeps	3–3.5 hrs	1–2 hrs	Peekaboo, cloth books, moving toys, dolls, moving more
10–12 months	Wakes at a similar time in morning and in a similar pattern at night	11–12 hours per night (no night feed required), 2 day sleeps	3–4 hrs	1–1.5 hrs	Music, stacking blocks, kitchen objects, playgroup

20

BIRTH TO 3 WEEKS

A HEALTHY baby between birth and three weeks old needs food, sleep and comfort. In this very new stage of your baby's life, it's all about getting to know each other. It's important to be aware of this because new parents are faced with a barrage of information on birth and parenting, the psychology of babies, rhythm and routine, health – it's a long list. The internet can be a dangerous place. Enter 'crying baby' into your search engine and you will get every response from 'it's normal' (most likely) to 'your baby might have a brain tumour' (most unlikely). Health professionals will give their advice; self-proclaimed professionals will write how-to books; and, of course, there are family and friends offering well-intentioned but thinly veiled advice on everything from cures for colic to long-winded stories on how things were 'in my day'.

Very quickly, parents become confused and frustrated about where to get the right information for them and their baby. If you feel that something is not right, you need to trust your instinct and act upon it. Otherwise, take a deep breath, slow things down and spend this precious early time getting to know your baby.

So, to the basics of sleeping and feeding. This period of about three weeks is the time you and your baby need to move from the dream to the reality of parenting. The baby becomes more alert at around three weeks but until then, she will sleep for a lot of the time. That's what she's meant to do. Does it really matter if she sleeps all snuggled up on you, in her bassinette or her pram? Not really. Yes, there is some structure that we need to be mindful of in order to give the baby what she needs but it doesn't matter where she gets it from. Allowing yourself time to let your instinct kick in will help you understand your baby's cues for food and sleep.

A very young baby will take up to an hour to feed and she will need six to eight feeds per day (remembering that in newborn world, a day is twenty-four hours long with no distinction between night and day). This means you will be sitting down for at least six to eight hours over a twenty-four hour period. Factor in nappy changes, settling and taking care of yourself, and you'll see what I mean about staying at home to settle in. If you are bottlefeeding, the length of each feed will be a little shorter. Babies exert most of their energy when they're feeding. They become very tired, very quickly. Their awake window is somewhere between forty-five minutes to an hour, depending on where and when you are feeding. When they're awake, they are gorgeous but they won't be up for peekaboo just yet so enjoy their cross-eyed attempts to focus and gummy mouth-moving.

Babies need to sleep regularly for a minimum of one and a half hours, up to three or three and a half hours. It's quite a deep sleep. If you have a newborn sleeping in the pram while you're in the kitchen doing odd jobs and you need to go out, often your baby will keep sleeping. This is because she is a newborn and she's exerted so much energy feeding that her body has to sleep in order to gain energy to feed again.

I call this the honeymoon period. But I also tell parents that it starts to change at about three weeks so, first, make the most of it and, second, get ready for change!

Very young babies tend to have an unsettled period each day, usually between two feeds, somewhere in the twenty-four hour window and mainly in the dark hours. There is no rhyme or rhythm to this but it usually means that over the course of the day, the baby has gradually become overstimulated and a little more tired as the day has progressed. Sometimes, even on the quietest of home days, it will happen. In the first ten days, it usually happens overnight and you'll think you're doing something wrong. You're not. This is normal behaviour in babies.

Because parents of newborns get tired, too, when their baby cries they feel they need to 'fix' it. Try not to. Just go to your baby and say something like this (in your most patient voice): 'Okay, little one, you just need me to cuddle you.' Go out to the sofa and *safely* settle in for some cuddle time, making sure you don't drop off to sleep. Make yourself a cup of tea and just ride it out. Long-term, your baby will settle better. You're not building a rod for your own back, this is something your baby needs (you) to do. If your baby is still

115

needing this at three to six weeks, I would be questioning why, but for now, it's fine. Whether you pat, rock or walk around with your baby, the settling technique is up to you. You need to try these things to see what works best for you and your baby.

CHEAT SHEET:
BIRTH TO 3 WEEKS

THINGS TO CONSIDER

The first ten days are considered the honeymoon period.

A 'day' is the whole 24-hour period.

Your baby doesn't know the difference between night and day.

Your baby may feed up to 10 times per day.

This is a time to get to know how to feed and handle your baby and adjust to life as a family.

SLEEP

Babies often sleep anywhere and well.

Most babies have an unsettled period every day.

It's important to keep sleep and settling simple and consistent.

Tired cues from your baby include restless body movements, whingeing and inability to relax.

SETTLING

Wrapping is very important as it quietens your baby's body for sleep.

It's okay to cuddle your baby to sleep at this age. Rocking and patting gently also help.

Babies are often unsettled overnight in the early weeks – hold your baby until she settles and then put her back into her bed.

WHAT DO BABIES NEED AT THIS AGE?

• Calmness and consistency

• Wrapping for settling and sleep

• Closeness to you

• Protection from people who are unwell or large crowded environments

RHYTHMIC PATTERN

• Your newborn will feed as little as 6 times and up to 10 times in 24 hours

• Usually awake for an hour (including the feed)

• Sleeps for 1.5–3 hours at a time

TIPS FOR PARENTS OF NEWBORNS

• Take each day at a time

• Work together as a couple and/or accept all offers of help

• Sleep when you can

• Eat well and exercise

• Try to keep a balance in your life

21

❧

3–6 WEEKS

A T about three weeks old, your baby will start to become more alert.

You're both coming out of that sleepy, getting-to-know-you birth to three-week window into a time when your baby has one of many growth spurts. You will start to get greater eye contact and your baby will begin to move her head from left to right much more easily. In general, your baby will begin to move around a lot more.

The good thing about this growth spurt is that babies who have been slow at feeding (I mean feeding well but taking a long time) will start to become a little more efficient and effective. This, in turn, seems to work with an irregular milk supply – things become more even and feeds are more predictable.

This growth spurt and heightened alertness sometimes meets with more difficult settling. Your baby's sleep patterns change and along with increased alertness comes more stimulation. It's a natural process but it requires a bit more work for everyone. Your baby has to learn to calm herself and work out an effective way of sleeping. Those first few weeks were spent sleeping off the fatigue of feeding and gaining energy for the next feed so settling was usually pretty straightforward. If you do have a really unsettled baby in the first three weeks, this is a pretty good indication that, excluding illness, you need to look at your feeding patterns, or that your baby might be becoming overtired.

The other reason is that your baby is growing up! With increased movement, you'll notice your baby isn't playing, as such. She's not oo-ing and goo-ing at a toy hanging in front of her, but she's just much more *actively* alert. She can move her body in a more controlled way; her eye movement is better and she can concentrate a little bit more. Her feeds are more effective. It's time to very, *very* gently help your baby to learn to self-settle.

This means you need to think about creating more *rhythm* in your baby's day. Note I say 'rhythm'. Parents can tend to get very confused about what a rhythm is, and often mistake it for a 'routine'. They are looking for the structure of a routine – a day that's timed, in place and something that's going to work. Every day. All the time. In reality, this doesn't happen. Sorry.

How will you know when all this is happening?

The shift out of the three-week honeymoon period can, weirdly, happen within about forty-eight hours of the baby turning three weeks old. Almost overnight, your baby will wake up for feeds, be more alert and may feed more efficiently.

And if you actually weigh and measure your baby around this time, you might find he has put on a good amount of weight and has also grown in length.

There are lots of different books out there that will tell you about growth patterns, but the traditional markers are around three weeks, six weeks and twelve weeks. There is always the steady growth of babies but these three stages are the well-known points where we would say that the baby is having a growth spurt. Something invariably changes at around these markers.

And then what?

At this 3–6 week stage, I encourage parents to gently place some sort of day/night rhythm into the baby's life. In this early period, it doesn't seem to make a big difference but, if you do it, by the time your baby reaches six to nine weeks old, you will be glad you persevered.

Another good reason to start working out a day/night rhythm is because about now, many partners will be heading back to work. Everyone is moving back into everyday life and often one parent is at home with the beginnings of a new life without as much help as there has been to date. In this new life, the easiest way to manage is to set up a few patterns so there is some predictability around your day.

Subtly, the environment around the baby needs to be changed. The easiest way to do this is to simply create day and night, that is, light and dark – this is what I mean by day/night rhythm. I use the daylight and night-time hours as a guide because we don't always start and end each day at the same time. Obviously, there needs to be flexibility with this since babies aren't robots and there are often other family members to consider. The important thing to remember is to work out what your baby needs and try to factor these things into day or night hours.

Babies who are three to six weeks old feed quite regularly; about every three to three and a half hours. Difficulties will arise if you set in your mind that your baby *will* feed every three hours, or four hours, for that matter. Babies are not that rigid – they can't be. They function from an instinct that says, 'I'm tired and I need to go to sleep' and/ or 'I'm hungry and I need to feed'. What you're doing is just bringing the environment in around them so that it becomes more rhythmic.

So what might your day be like?

Let's just go back a week or so. Your baby would have fed and most likely have fallen back to sleep. He *wanted* to go back to sleep. Other than being in an unsettled window, you would have most likely settled your baby without too much fuss.

Now that your baby is just that little bit older, he may have fed a little quicker, but instead of falling back to sleep, he may now be in a state of quiet alertness. He will be relaxed and looking around. He is not giving you the signal that he needs to go to sleep. You might put your baby down in a rocker while you make yourself a cup of tea. You need to be careful at this stage because, in the early part of this 3–6 week period, your baby's newfound curiosity for things and active alertness may not last for the entire cup of tea! I hear from many parents, 'I just kept him up for a couple of hours – he didn't seem to want to sleep!'

This is where you should think about what your baby *needs*. He might have been awake for an hour, including a forty-minute feed, and you might start to notice that his body is not as relaxed as it was straight after the feed. He now needs to go to bed. By the time the baby is yawning, crying and agitated, he is overtired and it will take much longer for him to go to sleep.

Generally speaking, the baby has been awake for the same amount of time between sleeps but his feeds are getting shorter and his periods of quiet alertness are getting longer. (Note here that 'awake' means, well, not asleep and 'alert' means taking in his surroundings and generally responding to you. This quiet alert time doesn't include the time when you're changing nappies or when he is showing tired signs and settling for sleep.) So, your baby has spent time taking in his environment and now, bless him, he's had enough fun for the moment and is ready to go to bed. Remember again; the length of awake time is not much different to a week or so ago, but he's just having a shorter feed and a longer alert time. The alert time alone is stimulating to your baby. You don't need to produce the bells and whistles, nor does your baby need television or any other type of 'education' while he is awake. All your baby needs is time with his parents; he wants to be close to you.

The flip side of this extra alert time is that you can get a few jobs done when the baby is awake. You can officially now have your breakfast and your cup of tea while chatting with your baby! He will be interested in watching you move while you eat and drink. To a baby, this is fascinating. Lap it up!

Being able to do a few jobs around the house brings a sense of achievement to a new parent. Some parents feel that as long as their baby's eyes are open, they must be right in front of him all the time. Not necessary. Your child needs to be in a safe environment, with all his needs met, including the feeling that you are not far away. Being on the floor in a bouncy chair is enough for him. Later, you might want to introduce some toys for your baby to look at but, for now, you having your breakfast and then putting a load of washing on is, in your baby's eyes, an Oscar-worthy performance.

Remember that during this time, your baby is still having six to eight feeds per day, most of which you will be giving him during daylight hours. By regularly staying close to your baby, but doing things other than holding him, you are assuring your baby that he will be okay if he isn't in your arms all the time. Sure, you will still give your baby lots of cuddles and if you are breastfeeding, you will share that physical closeness, but regular time in close proximity without touching is good for you both.

If you look at your day during this stage, you will most likely have five feed periods with four sleep cycles within that period. So, with all this feeding and parenting, how is your day likely to unfold?

The most important thing to remember is that whatever rhythm you start to introduce, you should think ahead to what your baby will be needing further down the track. One of the most important rhythms that you will be working towards is that your baby will need two sleeps per day at around twelve months of age. Those two daytime sleeps should be in a bed. This means when your baby is three to six weeks old, you need to start switching your arms for a bed.

The 'bed' could be the bassinette or perhaps the pram in another room in the house. A very simple sleep structure is being introduced here. That is, your baby will be tucked into his bed (pram, cot, bassinette) and moved to a quiet place to sleep. Essentially, you've taken your baby out of the light, sensory-filled area where he was awake for his feed to a darker, quieter place to sleep. Think about the phones ringing and the massive plasma television screen (is there any wonder your baby is staring at it – he is *gobsmacked* by the *light* of the screen, not the topic, trust me). You need to take him away from the bright lights and jarring noises so he can rest well.

Think about when you want to go to sleep. You have your night-time routine – you might have a warm shower, brush your teeth, slather promises on your face and crawl into bed to read before switching off the light. With your own routine, you are winding down from the day and preparing yourself for sleep. It's the same for your baby.

Settling down for a longer sleep

Your baby's room should be devoid of bright light. It doesn't need to be pitch black, but it needs to be closed down. Your baby needs to sleep in an environment that is comfortable, just as you do. If you want a nap on a Sunday afternoon, you would just flop onto the couch for twenty minutes and you'd be fine. For a baby, twenty minutes is *not* fine – well, not until they are much older. If you hopped into your bed on a Sunday afternoon, you might sleep for a couple of hours because the environment is different. It's warmer, darker and you associate your bed with deep rest. Again, same for your baby.

If you're at home, your baby's two sleeps per day might consist of one in the morning and the other in the afternoon. I'm not suggesting you dictate your day around this, but you should try to have two of the four sleep cycles in bed. The other two sleep cycles will probably happen during a window of time when you go out, such as when you duck out to pick up some shopping or meet a friend for a coffee. Try to make these trips between feeds and try *not* to be out for the whole day. Trust me on this one. Your baby will become overstimulated and we all now know what that means.

There is usually a cycle of sleep where the baby is unsettled – traditionally that's a late afternoon thing where the baby will cluster feed, be more wakeful and seem to not want to sleep. Cluster feeding is when your baby takes several shorter feeds over the course of the afternoon/early evening. The reason for this is because mums are often getting tired and their milk supply has reduced over the course of the day. This latter part of the day is when babies are also getting weary and their ability to feed well is reduced. There's nothing wrong with this, it's just how the day pans out for many mums and their babies. I will often suggest that this is a good time for parents to put the baby in the pram or pouch and head out for a short walk.

Over these three weeks, a rhythm starts to form between parents and the baby and life starts to change. Of course, you always get the extremes. There might be parents who never go out, instead wanting to stay at home for every sleep. And then there are parents who are always out and the baby will sleep anywhere and everywhere. These parents think that this will last for the long-term. But we know that further down the track, problems arise as a result of not staying home and allowing these early rhythms to form. Try to find a happy medium but, at the minimum, allow your baby to have two sleeps at home in the day.

Starting a new life with a baby is about finding the balance. It's *always* about finding the balance. And that's why, if you don't understand what your baby *needs*, the scales will always tip towards you because that's what you can control. *Your* needs will be met and you will struggle to find a rhythm with your baby because he has needs too – and ones that are not the same as yours! You can decide when to leave the house, where to go and so on, but you can't *control* your baby. You have to learn about his needs and create a rhythm so that you can co-exist happily.

Of course, there are many aspects of motherhood, particularly in the early days, which make you feel completely *out* of control! You have those rampaging hormones, you are probably lacking sleep and your life in general has been tipped upside down (in a good way!). It's important to remember that accepting this change is the first step to creating a new rhythm. This is the reality of parenthood.

Feeding

During this 3–6 week period, the average situation is where a mother is feeding at night, particularly if she is breastfeeding. Sure, for bottlefed babies or with a bottle of expressed breast milk, dads can get up to help. Feeds tend to be shorter although for breastfed babies, the feeds might still be long. There are many elements in terms of what constitutes a feed. Your baby is still very, very young. The change to parenthood is still very raw and you are still learning how to manage everything. Feeding and settling still hasn't become a fluent, fluid activity for you and your baby. If there are any clinical issues still going undiagnosed, you will be trying to manage those as well – by this I mean essentially breastfeeding. If there is any doubt about what is going on, you should get in touch with a lactation consultant as soon as you can.

You are still on a steep learning curve with your new baby. But remember, if your first thought is to consider your baby's needs, you can make better choices about what you have to do as a family. Each time I meet a family, I listen to their story but then we talk about *what their baby needs*. We talk about what their baby is doing in relation to what a baby generally needs at that particular age. I don't mean that they should *only* do what the baby needs. Having an understanding of the fundamentals means that parents can look at a whole day and see how everything can fit in. If they understand that a baby needs at least two sleep cycles in a bed, then perhaps when that Sunday christening is on the calendar, they might think about staying in that morning and making sure the baby has a good morning sleep in his bed, rather than heading out in the pram for breakfast down at the beach.

I'm not promoting a rigid routine, as many books out there do. Parenting doesn't work like that (well, it doesn't work very *well* like that because then there is no flexibility). We want flexible, calm babies but they need to *learn* how to do this and, as new parents, so do you. When you understand what your baby *needs*, you can implement different patterns throughout the day to signal when things are about to change.

Feed-bath-feed

For example, and I mentioned this earlier, during this 3–6 week period, your baby will be able to respond to a rhythm that teaches him about night and day. You might start a routine of things that you do at the end of every day. This routine will tell your baby that things are going to change (in this case, soon he is going into his bed for a big long sleep). This pattern is commonly known as feed-bath-feed.

This evening pattern is implemented somewhere in the vicinity between 5.30 pm and 7.30 pm – note, the window of time (two hours) *is* big when you start because, remember, your baby is still only about three weeks old and is not predictable (and won't be for a while yet). This window gets smaller over the following weeks as more predictability comes into your baby's day.

The feed-bath-feed pattern can involve a couple of different combinations. You can do one side of a breastfeed, then a bath, then the second side of the breastfeed. This combination does a couple of things. First, it makes sure your baby has fed well at this feed. Second, the latter part of the feed should be done in a quieter environment. This becomes a bit tricky when you have toddlers around or older kids needing help with homework, for example. But that's when you need to think about what your baby needs and then where it all fits within your family. And your family might have a number of aspects you'll need to take into consideration – trust me, there are a million and one variations!

However your family is structured, your baby is the littlest-link-with-the-loudest-voice and must have his needs met while still fitting in with everyone else. Hang in there – you'll manage!

Settling

You might be wondering why the window for the feed-bath-feed pattern is as long as two hours. It's because you need to try out what works best for you and your family. It could be that your baby has a breastfeed, then a bath, followed by a top-up via a bottle. It might be that your baby is formula-fed and you feed him the first part of the bottle before his bath so he is nice and relaxed, and afterwards you feed him the rest of his bottle. The important part of this pattern is that you do the feed after the bath in a quiet environment. You can take your baby to his room where you can turn the lights down and sit quietly together. This signals to your baby that something has changed in the rhythm of his day. Your baby learns that during the day he might be fed in the lounge room, cafe or cross-legged in the park, to now being fed in a familiar, quiet room and that means it's time for bed.

If your baby struggles to go off to sleep, try to stay in his quiet, darkened room. You may well need to help your baby, but resist getting up to go for a walk to settle him. He doesn't need to say goodnight to the birds and the owls and the stars (this will only stimulate him). You may need to hold or rock your baby and soothe him with your voice, but do this in his room.

Let me just go back for a moment to the time when your baby was under three weeks old. The signal for your baby to settle was wrapping. It didn't matter if you put your baby down to sleep, cuddled him or put him into his bed; that time was more about getting to know your baby and helping to quieten his body by wrapping. Now that your baby is between three and six weeks old, you're going to add another layer onto the signal to settle. Now you are not only wrapping your baby, you are putting him down to sleep. Remember, very few people go to sleep in an upright position with the fairies coming to put them into bed. Being a practical person, I'm not going to tell you that it's perfectly fine to rock your baby to sleep for the first six months, because undoing that is going to be so much more difficult for both parent and child.

If you understand the stages that your baby reaches where he can settle himself, and you then implement another layer onto your settling pattern, it is much easier for your baby to learn to go off to sleep by himself when he gets older. This stage is about your baby getting used to being put down to sleep; more often than not, while he's still awake. If your baby is calm and relaxed, he will often stay this way for about fifteen to twenty minutes before going to sleep. Some babies will drop off to sleep sooner, while others will call out and still need help to go off to sleep.

Helping your baby to go off to sleep

Initially, if your baby calls out to you, leave him in the bed. You might body rock, gently pat or quietly shush your baby (or all of the above). Try to comfort your baby while he is in his bed. However, if he just protests within that window of time, pick him up, comfort and settle him and then put him back into bed, awake, and go back to the same steps as you started with. Doing this sets up a pattern of consistency: I've wrapped you, cuddled you and now I'm going to put you into bed to sleep. You're letting your baby know that it is okay to be lying in his bed by himself; he is not being abandoned and you will comfort him, but it's time to go to sleep. It may take you three, four or five rounds of this settling pattern, and each time you pick up your baby, you should comfort him until he is calm.

Again, I'm coming back to one of my biggest messages – that is, your baby needs time and patience. What often happens is that parents feel very short on time. Many parents don't make dinner for themselves until the baby is asleep so they're trying to get the baby to sleep so they can eat and have time together. This is where a bit of outside help comes in handy. Ask or arrange for someone to drop a meal in so you can take the time you and your baby need to settle him off to sleep *and* you don't have to worry about dinner.

What happens when your baby is not having any of it?

When I talk with parents that have had quite a good day but then their baby is consistently unsettled towards the end of that day, often I ask what they've been doing to settle the baby. The story is a familiar one. Parents will tell me that they started off wrapping, settling and putting the baby into bed. After a period of trying to settle the baby, many parents say they decided to take the baby downstairs to their partner to 'have a go' at settling. Sometimes they'll change the baby's nappy in the living room, warm a bottle or try a number of other techniques to soothe her. The main problem here is that the baby's environment is changing every five minutes. You need to keep the environment the same. This means staying in the quiet bedroom and, most importantly, you and your partner need to be doing *the same thing*. You have to communicate with each other.

Dad (or mum) might be out at work all day and whoever comes home to the one who has been with the baby needs to know what is working (or not). I know it's sometimes hard because both of you are tired and you want to eat dinner and catch up, but first you need to have a quick chat about what's going on with the baby. Doing this will keep the settling technique consistent and this is key. Dads, if you take over the settling on Friday night when your partner nips out for a catch-up with the girls, hit the record button on Friday Night Footy and settle that baby the way your partner has been doing all day. Not only will you get your baby to sleep more successfully, you'll catch the entire game, have a rested baby and a happy partner.

The conversations about baby settling that I have with parents always return to the same point. It's part of the reality of being a parent. You aren't two single people sharing your lives anymore. You are a family with a child that has needs and relies on you to meet those needs. You must be able to communicate with each other about these needs.

I recently got a call from a lovely couple whose evenings consisted of settling their daughter. That's it – and often from 6 pm until late. When I arrived, the evening was in full swing as usual. Both parents were handing the baby to each other, trying to work out what would be the most successful settling technique. My suggestion was to wrap the baby, take her to her room, put her into bed, turn out the lights and gently rock her body. She eventually went to sleep. Yes, we had to go back into her room two or three times, but she went to sleep. Her environment remained the same and the settling technique was the same each time we went in to her. Both parents saw that what they had been doing was inconsistent to the baby and created further stimulation, rather than quiet.

Let's face it. To learn anything, you need to do it over, and over, and over again. In babyland, that's about three to five days in a learning sequence. It's doing it about twenty times. It's why we don't see new rhythms falling into place until about the third or fourth day. Parents need to be told this. If parents know it is going to take this amount of time to implement change in their baby's life, then I think they would be more consistent. I honestly believe parents don't think 'it's all about me'. They really want what is good and right for their baby. They just get flustered when things aren't working as quickly as they'd like, and usually that's after the first or second attempt at something. When parents start being consistent, this is when things start to settle down.

The message for partners here is this: I know when you come home from work you want to be a great parent. I know you want to join in with the family goings-on and you're (mostly) busting to hold your new baby. It's a great thing to want to be a hands-on parent. Honestly, it is. However . . . the best thing that you can do when you get home is to say to your partner, 'How are you?' and/or 'Where are we up to?' Believe me, your partner will relax quickly if she knows you are continuing on from whatever has been working for her all day. There will be time for new experiences when your baby is older. In these early days and weeks, it's about settling the baby down for the night.

It's also about communication. But you can't communicate your baby's needs if you don't know what they are. If you understand what your baby needs, then you'll understand better the idea of being consistent. When I see parents in this 3–6 week stage, I offer this little story:

What would you do if your child came home from kindergarten and insisted that 'one plus one equals four'? You'd be concerned, wouldn't you? You'd probably go to the kitchen and get two of something, say, oranges. You'd say, 'Here's one orange, and here's another orange. How many oranges?' When your child says, 'Four', you then say, 'No, one orange, plus another orange. How many oranges?' And over you go with it until the penny drops.

Obviously there will be an expectation at this point that your child knows a bit about numbers and counting, but again, it's about the consistency of teaching and learning and your child finally understanding and doing.

So for the night-time routine it's:

1. Feed
2. Bath
3. Feed
4. Bed

Very basically, that's it.

The fundamental rule is that your baby needs the basis of a pattern in order for her to learn to sleep.

There are, however, some babies that will shut their eyes and go to sleep as soon as they are put into bed. These babies make up a *very low* percentage of three- to six-week-olds. There are also babies that will struggle to settle no matter what you do. Research is ongoing about why these babies really struggle. You occasionally hear of parents saying their baby doesn't need 'much' sleep. I always find this challenging to accept since babies need sleep to thrive. Eventually, issues arise and, in my opinion, it's usually due to an overtired baby.

Parents get confused because there is a lot of information floating around about what your baby needs, how much and when. The only way your baby can learn is with consistent patterns of behaviour. In this 3–6 week stage, it doesn't matter whether she is sleeping in a bed or a bassinette or in the pram. It *does* matter that your baby is given the chance to sleep in the right environment. And it does matter that she gets the right *signals* to sleep. All of this is just about communication. Whether it's with your partner when he or she gets home from work, whether you're visiting family and you're telling them what stage you're at with your baby – it's about communication and adjusting to your new life as a family.

CHEAT SHEET:
3–6 WEEKS

THINGS TO CONSIDER

FEEDING

- More alert after feeds

- More efficient at feeding

- Day/night rhythm forming

SLEEP

Babies will still need you to be with them when settling and may also need you to help them resettle.

During the day, at least two sleeps should be in bed to encourage good long-term sleep behaviour.

Most babies have an unsettled period each day and an unsettled day each week. Be patient and seek help if you have several unsettled days in a row.

SETTLING

Wrap your baby.

Cuddle until calm.

Put your baby down awake (he will still need you to help him get to sleep).

If unsettled, try to settle him while he is in bed for a few minutes. I suggest rocking, patting, or offering a dummy until calm. This may take a few minutes.

If your baby is still unsettled, pick him up until he is calm and then put him back to bed. This process could take a few minutes. Be patient, consistent and with time, your baby will settle.

WHAT DO BABIES NEED AT THIS AGE?

FEEDING

• Babies are more alert

• Still feeding around the clock

• May be loosely forming a day/night pattern – e.g. he may feed 5 times during the day and 2–3 times overnight

SLEEP

Awake cycle (feed and alert awake time) in the day is 1 hour 15 minutes to 1 hour 30 minutes.

During the day, sleep cycle may decrease to 1 hour 30 minutes from 2 to 2 hours 30 minutes.

Late afternoon/early evening may be a time of unsettled behaviour.

Night rhythm of feed-bath-feed can be done at this stage.

Offer first breast or half bottle, bath, then second breast or remainder of bottle in a quiet room and put your baby to bed (I usually suggest trying this when a feed is due between 5.30–7.30 pm).

RHYTHMIC PATTERN

At this stage, your baby is too young to have a predictable routine but you are still able to seek a gentle rhythm between you and your baby. Simply, it is daytime in daylight hours and night-time in the dark!

At 3 weeks, the awake cycle is around 1 hour to 1 hour 15 minutes.

At 6 weeks, the awake cycle is around 1 hour 15 minutes to 1 hour 30 minutes.

At this stage, mothers are feeling better after delivery and are thinking about getting out and about. Your balance should be between what your baby needs and going out to get things done.

This gentle pattern below can be adapted to fit lots of different family needs. The basis is that babies at this age will generally feed every 3–3.5 hours.

SUGGESTED DAILY RHYTHM

MORNING FEED

• Awake period 1 hour to 1 hour 30 minutes, (includes feed and alert period, eye to eye contact, talking, gentle rocking)

• Morning sleep, minimum 1 hour 30 minutes, in bed (this sleep generally continues until about 14 months)

MID-MORNING FEED

• Awake again for around 1 hour to 1 hour 30 minutes – maybe cuddles and a little time on the floor with you close by

• Another sleep, 1 hour 30 minutes or more – perhaps in the pram/car/sling while you have energy to go out and get things done (this sleep generally continues until about 6–7 months)

LUNCH-TIME FEED

• Awake period 1 hour to 1 hour 30 minutes

• Longer sleep 1 hour 30 minutes to 2 hours 30 minutes in bed (this afternoon sleep usually continues until about 3 years)

AFTERNOON FEED

• Generally an unsettled or wakeful period (baby may catnap in 40-minute windows)

• Baby may cluster feed

• Afternoon – generally an unsettled or wakeful period – baby may catnap in 40-minute windows, or may cluster feed

EVENING FEED

• Evening – feed-bath-feed routine can be done when a feed is due, between 5.30 and 7.30 pm, then bed

OVERNIGHT

• Feeds and sleep

22

6–12 WEEKS

PARENTS of babies that are six to twelve weeks old tell me this story a lot: 'We've been taking him out with us since he was a newborn but now when we go out, he cries all the time! What do we do?'

Up until their babies are about six weeks old, parents don't get a lot of information. Yes, they get information about taking the baby home and what to do in those initial days and they form an idea of what they want their babies to do as they get older, but this 6–12 week period is the window where things can go awry, and because each baby is unique, things can change quickly or slowly. It can be a confusing time. In the first six weeks, babies feed and sleep. They can be comforted by rocking or patting and we don't put a lot of emphasis on where they go to sleep. From three to six weeks, it's a good idea to start putting a day/night pattern into place while the relationship between parents and baby is developing. But at around six weeks, there's a growth spurt and things can change.

By six weeks, feeding and settling is becoming more predictable and efficient. Mothers will be coming out of the 'fog' of the first few weeks of having a baby. Parents are feeling a bit more confident and your baby will finish feeds with lots of gummy, milky smiles. If you and your baby are struggling with feeding, make sure you get some professional help as soon as possible.

With this increase in feeding efficiency comes even more alertness. The gentle day/night patterns you've implemented in the previous 3–6 week period will help you to understand your baby's cues for food and sleep. This is going to be very helpful because your baby's awake time will start to get a little longer and you'll have to be on the ball as far as her need for sleep is concerned. This 6–12 week period brings with it a more curious baby who is beginning to react to her environment. Your baby can see further, taking in a lot more of her surroundings, such as trees moving outside, light, music and general noises around her. Up until now, the environment has been a fairly minor factor affecting the baby's behaviour, whether it be feeding, awake and looking around or sleeping. Now it's important.

A six- to twelve-week-old baby's awake window is somewhere between an hour and a quarter and an hour and a half. By twelve weeks it will be a fairly constant hour and a half, at which point parents have a good opportunity to start putting into place a predictable pattern for the baby where she will react to what it is that she needs.

Being more alert means being more reactive to the environment. And just like you and me, our environment predicts how well our day will go. If we're overstimulated we can get really harassed and nothing seems to fall into place. If everything's fallen into line in a predictable pattern, give or take a little bit of time, then we feel more relaxed and we move through our day better. Babies are exactly the same, except that babies need us as adults to help them go through these stages.

At this stage, whoever is at home looking after the baby is starting to gain confidence about their ability to parent. If we're talking about mum, she's getting used to the idea of not leaving home to go to work every day. This increased confidence needs a little gentle reminder. In another life, increased confidence and greater ability usually means taking on more. When you're looking after a baby, you need to watch this. Loading yourself up with more and more activities, social gatherings and general expectations is a recipe for disaster. This early time is still new, regardless of how long you feel like you've been doing it. This stage should still be about the baby. Remember, she's only forty-two days old! Take it easy and enjoy the transition.

What does your baby need?

Despite increasing alertness, your baby is not quite ready to be entertained, as such. There's an awful lot you can buy for your baby but, really, she doesn't need much more than a mat on the floor and for you to be close by. Get down on the floor and talk quietly to your baby and play with her hands and toes. Make faces and laugh. If you feel like a goose, then by all means read something but be present and keep it simple. If it's a beautiful day, take the mat outside and lie together looking at the trees.

Babies that are six to twelve weeks old need feeding every three to four hours. It's still really frequently during the day, but the time between feeds will begin to extend at night. During the day, if your baby is feeding every three to three and a half hours, she is likely to be awake for about an hour and a half and then sleep for somewhere between an hour and a half to two hours. Can you see the decrease of long sleeping patterns during the day? So, roughly, if you took a day as being from 6–7 am to 6–7 pm, babies have five feeds and four sleep periods. Again, I suggest that two of those sleep periods are in the baby's bed in a room. The other two can fit in with whatever you have to do – perhaps a nap in the car on the way to get groceries.

Crying

Crying is your baby's way of saying, 'I need you.' Familiarity and comfort are very important for a baby. Babies need steady transitions and *time* to get used to things.

If you look at a cohort of people, I doubt many would run 5 kilometres, arrive home, have a shower and hop into bed. It's incomprehensible to go from being really busy or active and then suddenly dropping off to sleep (unless you are medically inclined). Unbelievably, this is what we sometimes ask babies to do. Busy, busy, busy, now put your head down and go to sleep. Babies need to be slowed right down before bed. Adults have their habits and patterns – you clean your teeth, go to the loo, hop into bed and perhaps read for a while before you turn out the light and go to sleep. If this pattern is interrupted, I'm guessing you feel like something's not quite right; you get up again, fiddle around for a while until you're happy everything's right, then go back to bed.

For young babies, the busyness of family life can be a bit chaotic. I can always pick it when a mother says, 'I just can't get her to sleep at the end of the day.' When I ask the mother what she's been doing during the four hours before bed, the answer is often: 'Oh well, I just had to take the kids to and from ballet class and after that we quickly ran over and did a bit of shopping and then I got home, cooked dinner and then I fed the baby.' That is a lot for a baby to cope with.

Sometime the *whole* family needs to slow down. Older siblings need to understand that their new baby sister or brother will not cope with a lot of racing around, shouting, tears and overtiredness (from them and their parents!). Instead of doing six things a week with them, perhaps cut it back to one activity each until the baby is older. It's about balance.

For a first baby, it's about the parents slowing down. Often, the stay-at-home parent is trying to negotiate how to stay at home having probably never really done so. My suggestion for a day is usually something like this:

- For the first sleep cycle of the day, stay at home and let the baby have a good sleep in bed.
- From mid morning to lunch time, go and have a coffee with your friends.
- In the afternoon, put your baby back down in his bed for a sleep.
- In the late afternoon, when your baby might be unsettled, perhaps go for another walk.

Confidence and the mothers' group!

Unfortunately, babies do not arrive with a big batch of confidence for their parents. I'm not just referring to the ability to believe in yourself when it comes to making decisions about your baby, it's also about being able to hold your own amongst other parents, your own family – anyone, really. Most people have an anecdote to share about parenting or 'advice' they just can't help giving you. Some people are outright rude about their views on your parenting; some are passively aggressive.

Let me give you an example. Many new mothers like to meet for coffee, lunch, playgroup – lots of things. This is great but sometimes these get-togethers can become a bit of a posse. In the beginning, everyone meets at the early childhood centre and a mothers' group forms. You meet regularly for about four weeks and then you're all left to your own devices. Suddenly, what was once a group of new parents wading through early parenthood becomes a group of fairly fatigued individuals in this 6–12 week stage; navigating babies doing all sorts of different things. Friendly chats can become passive competitions about who is doing what. I know this doesn't always happen but, as for every party, there's always one!

If or when this happens, you need to gather your one-liners, based, of course, on what you and your baby need. If you don't want to join in during times when you'd rather have your baby at home, say something like, 'Thanks for asking us but it's sleep time at home – hope you all have a great time – maybe we could meet one morning for coffee next week?' If someone is commenting on what you are doing with your baby, you could reply, 'We're doing what works best for our family', and if you find yourself embedded in a group whinge about your partners, try to resist joining in and perhaps say, 'Maybe we're all just in neutral at the moment – it'll pass.' Whatever you say, say it with confidence and remember that you don't have to explain yourself to anyone. The 6–12 week period is a time when everyone is pretty tired and in the haze of new parenthood; you can find yourself saying and doing things you wouldn't normally breathe to anyone. Be forgiving and try to unleash that sense of humour – you will work out who you want to remain friends with and who you can happily live without.

As your baby reaches twelve weeks old, nights should be getting far more predictable. You are probably still giving your baby two feeds overnight. If your baby feeds well, he will generally sleep well. More good news is that parents generally start to feel much better because you're actually getting better quality sleep. You're even using the definition of night as between, say, seven o'clock in the evening until six in the morning – not whenever you go to bed and whenever you get up!

Some parents swear by a 'dream feed' just before midnight; others say it never works. Babies do a lot of growing in this period but you still need to keep giving them the chance to do it. This means that during the day, babies need their proper (bed) sleeps because the less sleep they get in the day, the more your nights will fall apart. Check with any sleep expert and they will tell you that sleep begets sleep. The more sleep your baby gets in the day, the better the sleep will be at night. The less sleep your baby gets in the day, the more difficult the sleep will be at night. And if it doesn't fall apart in the first few weeks, I can almost guarantee it will fall apart in the first few months.

In this 6–12 week period, babies need a *predictable* pattern of sleep with your help to teach them to sleep and resettle if necessary. Once you get a baby who *does* sleep, everyone is much happier. The persistence and patience it takes is worth it.

Wrapping

You should still be wrapping your baby since he hasn't matured to a point where he can quieten his body. Everybody who tells me their baby goes to sleep really well without being wrapped in this 6–12 week period also tells me their babies don't sleep very long, because as soon as they startle they wake themselves up again. So wrapping is still important. Cuddling to calm is still happening but it's important to allow your baby to learn to self-settle. Cuddle your baby until he is calm, which could be one minute, it could be ten minutes, but cuddle him until he is calm and put him in bed awake. Your baby is learning that he goes to bed awake and then shuts his eyes to sleep, not the other way around. The obvious problem with cuddling your baby to sleep is that when he wakes and you're not there, he doesn't know how to resettle himself.

If your baby wakes and becomes upset, pick him up, give him a cuddle until he is calm again and then put him back down in his bed again. You're telling your baby that you are here with him, but it's time for sleep. Whether that's rocking, patting, a dummy, a pick-up, a cuddle and then put down, that's okay.

Children are all about consistency and persistence, not about one day. Nobody learns anything in half a minute; remember it takes babies three to five days or at least twenty experiences. So you've got to give your baby time, but you need to keep it simple too. Persistence and patience is key.

CHEAT SHEET:
6–12 WEEKS

Note: These are just examples of rhythms for this stage. I have divided the day into morning, mid morning, lunch time, afternoon and evening, rather than prescriptive times, as I find this helps parents to identify parts of the day and establish rhythms. Babies will generally start their day at around 6–7 am. From there, just work with the suggested rhythm.

THINGS TO CONSIDER
Awake for periods of 1 hour 15 minutes to 1 hour 30 minutes during the day – often stay awake for 1.5 hours.
Babies are more alert and interested in their environment.
They don't need a lot of stimulation such as time on baby play mats with dangling toys.
At this stage, babies enjoy:
• time in a bouncy chair not far from parents
• tummy time
• being held closely; studying faces
• being on a mat in the backyard or park, watching the sky or movement in the trees
• going for a walk

SLEEP

At this age, I often see babies starting to wake at the 45-minute cycle. They need assistance to get back to sleep. This takes time and patience.

Babies often become 'top heavy' in sleep in that as the day goes on, they have less sleep and are often overtired by the end of the day. This makes them more unsettled, harder to get to sleep and less able to feed well.

SETTLING

• Generally still wrapped to help quieten their bodies

• Cuddle until calm

• Put to bed

• Maybe gentle body rocking or patting until sleepy, this may take up to 5 mins

• Leave the room

• You may need to repeat this a few times until your baby goes to sleep

SUGGESTED DAILY RHYTHM AT 6 WEEKS

MORNING

• 6–7 am feed

• Awake cycle 1 hour 15 minutes to 1 hour 30 minutes

• Sleep in bed, anywhere between 1 hour 30 minutes and 2 hours 30 minutes. Resettling may be needed

MID MORNING

• 9–10 am feed

• Awake cycle 1 hour 15 minutes to 1 hour 30 minutes

• Sleep in bed, anywhere between 1 hour 30 minutes and 2 hours 30 minutes – you may want to go out after this feed as your energy levels may be higher. It's okay for your baby to sleep in a pram while you go for a walk or do some shopping.

LUNCH TIME

• 12–1 pm feed

• Awake cycle 1 hour 15 minutes to 1 hour 30 minutes

• Sleep in bed, anywhere between 1 hour 30 minutes and 2 hours 30 minutes

AFTERNOON

• 3–4 pm feed

• Awake cycle 1 hour 15 minutes to 1 hour 30 minutes

• Afternoon sleep may well be shorter as babies are often more wakeful and unsettled at this time. Try going out for a walk with your baby in the pram or pouch.

EVENING

• 6–6.30 pm feed-bath-feed then bed

WHAT DO BABIES NEED AT THIS AGE?

During this 6–12 week stage, your baby needs more of a consistent day/night pattern to help extend night sleep.

Feeding is more efficient and feed length times may decrease.

Babies are more alert after feeds and begin to play and engage.

SLEEP

• Sleeping better at night after a feed-bath-feed pattern.

• Fewer unsettled nights.

• Parents are feeling more confident.

• Mum and baby are finding a rhythm to their day.

• A familiar pattern for the evenings is emerging.

• Babies are a little calmer in the evening.

• Two sleep cycles in a bed during the day. Babies sleep longer in a quiet and dimly lit room during the day.

RHYTHMIC PATTERN

At around 6 weeks, I suggest starting an evening routine – not routine by time, but more by the fact that it is in the evening and therefore distinguishing the difference between day and (the approach of) night.

Generally, it will be somewhere in the time frame between 6 pm to 7–7.30 pm where a feed may fall.

The sequence is feed-bath-feed. Many professionals advise a plan of rhythm in the evening and depending on the type of feeding, it can take many forms, including:

• First side of breast – bath – second side of breast; or

• Full breastfeed – bath – bottle top-up (expressed breast milk or formula); or

• One-third bottled formula – bath – two-thirds bottled formula.

With any evening rhythm, the second part of the feed should be done in a quiet (less stimulating) environment to help your baby be more restful.

At around 12 weeks, parents are often struggling with their baby waking after a 45-minute sleep cycle. I often suggest concentrating on the two longer morning and afternoon bed sleeps as these are the ones that the babies continue with. Resettling is important.

If resettling your baby is not working after 3 to 5 days, try speaking with your early childhood centre, trusted friend or professional mothercraft nurse, as fixing this at a young age leads to better long-term sleep.

This can be a difficult time and patterns will change. When speaking with mums, I look at the family needs including school runs and other commitments. It's a good time to talk about the needs of the whole family but, in the end, the baby is the one that needs consistency and the chance to sleep in a familiar environment.

23

3–6 MONTHS

I F you thought your baby was getting more alert in the 6–12 week period, wait until this 3–6 month period. It's a lovely time – full of smiles and gurgles. But this alertness means you need to stay on top of your baby's sleep needs, because while there's lots of fun to be had when he's awake, he can easily become overtired.

The lead up to this period is about teaching your baby to self-settle and putting in day/night patterns. It's important to persist with whatever is working for you and your baby. At this stage, the confidence parents have gained can also take a hit. After all the work you've put in, your inquisitive little baby decides he'd like to stay awake a little longer and you seem to be having a sleep battle. You're not seeing the quick results you were getting used to and your confidence gets a little shaky. When I meet parents in this 3–6 month period, it's nearly always about finding a balance for parents *and* baby so that both parties' sleep rhythms don't fall apart.

I always tell parents that between three and four and a half months there is going to be a lot of work helping the baby to self-settle and for the baby to be able to go into a sleep phase and then resettle itself. Often the baby will sleep for forty-five minutes, wake up and struggle to go back to sleep. As the baby becomes more overtired, sleep periods drop down to forty minutes, then down to twenty minutes, and soon you have a napper, not a sleeper. The baby who only sleeps for twenty to forty minutes is overtired.

The reason babies get overtired at this age is, dare I say it, universal. Parents have just got a good day/night pattern going and both parent and baby are getting some pretty good quality sleep at night. There is a growing confidence in parents that they will be able to settle their baby anywhere and a tendency to forget how tired a baby gets with compromised sleep. The desire to do a few more things each day tips the need scales in their direction a little too far and the baby starts to get overtired. I feel for parents at this stage because they've worked hard and when things get a little unbalanced, they get upset and frustrated.

I'm happy to say things get better around the 5–6 month mark because the baby *can* stay up a lot longer and there are longer gaps between sleeps for parents to be out and about. *But things only get better if you slow down a bit in this 3–6 month period and get back to basics with your baby's sleep patterns.*

Parents need to work together

This chapter is heavily skewed towards parental cooperation! It's always important but this period of time can be tricky on parents, so bear with me.

If a baby learns a pattern in, say, three to five days (Monday to Friday) and then suddenly their pattern changes tack on the next two consecutive days (Saturday and Sunday), it stands to reason that things will fall apart and those three to five days of learning have to start again.

When parents see me with a baby who's three to six months old, the first thing I do is have a chat about what their life is like. It's good to find a balance and show them how that balance can pan out over the next twelve months. Putting your baby's needs before yours for the first year of her life is a huge commitment but one that is definitely worthwhile. Relationships can become strained because each one is trying to fit in with the other. Whoever is at home with the baby is working hard to get sleep patterns going and when the weekend comes around, whoever is working all week wants to get out and about! You most definitely need to understand that a baby does not know when it's the weekend; she only knows that just when things seem to be getting rhythmic by Friday, there's chaos for two days. And then the mop up begins on a Monday morning! I'm not suggesting you both stay at home all weekend, but a sleep-in until nine o'clock, then out for breakfast followed by a walk on the beach might be tricky if your baby wakes at six o'clock and needs a sleep in bed at seven-thirty. Just go out for brunch instead. Or invite a couple of friends to your place for an easy dinner instead of going out.

In this 3–6 month period, there are lots of ups and downs and plenty of 'Are we doing the right thing?' and 'Why are we doing it?'. Persistence and patience with your day/night patterns is really important. Consistency works. But the same pattern or rhythm is not for every family; the consistency needs to be right for yours.

So even though I say the same thing about consistency and sleep patterns each time I see a parent with a three- to four-month-old baby, every one will be a bit different because I have to factor in what parents can cope with. What is their lifestyle? Do they have other children? What is the makeup of this particular family? What can they be consistent with?

I do know that there are some really, really difficult babies out there for whatever reason, and there are some really, really easy babies too. But the bulk of the babies are in the middle and need some guidance and, as parents, you are the ones that have to do it.

But here is the thing: whatever you do, you have to do it consistently and that takes communication between parents. If one parent wants to settle the baby by patting for five minutes and the other thinks it's better to walk around singing, the baby just gets confused. Whatever you decide to do, think carefully about what will work long-term for parents and baby – because when you get tired walking around, bad luck, you're committed. Of course, the reality of this is that you stop walking around and you change your method of settling, not because the baby won't settle, it's because your legs are tired and you want to rest as well! Work out what you can both do consistently and stick with it.

The conversation

My job is not to tell parents that what they're doing is *wrong* although I won't hold back making suggestions if I think it can help your family!

The conversation always begins with the basics of what the baby needs first and then we work out family schedules, hobbies, work and so on. We create a basic daily rhythm that starts when the baby wakes up in the day and finishes when the baby goes to bed at night. There's room for variance since the household is made up of humans, not machines! Most babies will wake up between 6 am and 7 am and most babies will need to be in their bed for a longer and restful sleep by 6.30–7.30 pm. Often the stay-at-home parent will say, 'But I want the baby to stay up until eight o'clock so my partner can see him.' My response to that is: 'Well, your partner needs to come home earlier because the baby can't stay awake longer.'

Couples are often trying to define themselves as a family and some have nowhere to start. The best place is to begin with where the baby's at and where they're heading to, so that parents can actually see that the work they're doing here at three months will lead to where they're going to be at six months. In the grand scheme of life, a few months is a short time, but it is a lot of work because the essence of what we're doing is settling and resettling in this window and usually establishing solid foods. There's a lot of repetition and, as much as you love your baby, I know it can be mind-numbing at times.

Your three-month-old baby usually has a good day/night pattern. She is much more alert and probably starting to be quite active with her hands. She might bring a toy to her mouth and suck on it to amuse herself. She may even be attempting a very basic roll where if she's on her front she might roll to her back. She's not intentionally rolling so enjoy her look of surprise when it happens. Your baby is still learning to self-settle and usually requires some resettling at sleep times.

The great thing about three-month-old babies is their nights are usually getting better. They're starting to sleep longer for maybe a five to six hour window somewhere overnight. The downside of this is that parents often think their baby needs *less* sleep. The reality is that babies need the same amount of sleep, it's just configured differently. At this age, there's more sleep at night and only two sleeps during the day.

If your baby reaches six months and she is not having a longer sleep at night, it is usually because you are feeding to settle her. We need to work out how much and when you're feeding. For instance, if you've fed your baby between six and seven o'clock at night and she wakes at nine o'clock, my guess is she doesn't need a feed, she needs to be resettled. If your baby is continually waking around nine o'clock, you might need to review the 6.00–7.00 pm feed to make sure she is feeding well with ample opportunity to have as much as she needs. In other words, don't rush the feed, despite whatever else may be happening in your household! Otherwise, keep persisting with settling.

Feeding

At three months, your baby needs about five feeds in the day; these are sucking feeds. It would be very rare for a three-month-old baby to be starting solids. 'Solids' is just the term we use to describe anything other than milk. Introducing solids into your baby's diet is a gradual process of increasing foods according to texture, density and amount. You might read that solids will help a baby to sleep longer. In fact, it makes absolutely no difference whatsoever to the baby's behaviour. This is because, first, a three-month-old can't eat enough for it to make a difference to sleep and, second, if you overfeed your baby, she will just wake up in discomfort. Times have changed since your grandmother's day when young babies were given condensed milk to 'fill up'!

As your baby grows beyond three months to around five or six months, you will begin to see signs that she is ready to try solid foods. Go to the chapter Solids to read more about this transition.

In the meantime, enjoy your little baby at this lovely age. It's a lot of work, but as I keep saying, it's well worth the effort to get good sleeping habits underway for when life gets *really* busy!

CHEAT SHEET:
3–6 MONTHS

Note: These are just examples of rhythms and times for this stage. Babies will generally start their day at around 6–7 am. From there, just work with the rhythm below.

3 MONTHS
Awake for periods of 1 hour 30 minutes during the day, with around 4 sleeps per day.
FEEDING
• 4–5 milk feeds per day
• Still 1–2 feeds overnight but dropping closer to one (generally by 4 months)
SLEEP
• 2 sleeps in bed, each for 1 hour 30 minutes to 2 hours
• 2 catnaps
Evening routine established at this stage – note that reading can be overstimulating to an overtired baby during the evening routine. Reading is important, but do it when your baby is alert and not needing to go to sleep.
SUGGESTED DAILY RHYTHM
6 am feed/play

7.30 am sleep in bed, try to resettle to get about 1 hour 30 minutes

9–10 am feed/play

45-minute catnap, sleep may shorten while out so remember that they may need to go to bed straight after next feed

12.30–1 pm feed

1–1.30 pm sleep in bed, sleep 2 to 2 hours 30 minutes (minimum 1 hour 30 minutes)

4–4.30 pm feed

20-minute catnap

6–6.30 pm feed-bath-feed then bed

5 MONTHS

Awake for periods of 1 hour 45 minutes to 2 hours during the day, with around 3 sleeps per day.

FEEDING

- 4 milk feeds per day

- 1 solids meal

- Often only having one feed overnight

SLEEP

- 2 sleeps in bed, each for 1 hour 30 minutes to 2 hours

- 1 catnap

Enjoys evening routine and knows what is coming next.

Night sleeping is usually much better with one long and a shorter sleep overnight.

SUGGESTED DAILY RHYTHM

6 am feed

7.45 am sleep in bed

9.30 am feed

11.15 am – 12 pm catnap (this sleep is shortening)

1 pm feed

1.30–2 pm sleep in bed

4.30 pm solids meal

6 pm bath

6.30 pm feed then bed

6 MONTHS

Awake cycle 2 hours to 2 hours 30 minutes during the day, with 2 sleeps per day.

FEEDING

• 4 milk feeds per day

• 2–3 solids meals

SLEEP

- 2 sleeps in bed, each for 1 hour 30 minutes to 2 hours

- One catnap for 15–20 minutes, usually mid-morning

SUGGESTED DAILY RHYTHM

6 am feed

7 am solids meal

8 am sleep in bed

10 am feed

12 pm catnap for 15–20 minutes

1.30 pm feed

2 pm sleep in bed

4.30 pm solids meal

6 pm bath

6.30 pm feed then bed (can often stay awake until around 7-ish)

24

6–9 MONTHS

GENERALLY speaking, parents of babies who are six to nine months old are feeling much more at ease. They're in a rhythmic pattern regardless of what that rhythmic pattern is and there's a lot of focus on the baby's gross motor developments, such as sitting, rolling, crawling, hand-to-hand, taking a toy from one hand and putting it into the other, and so on.

There's also a lot of focus on food. Food development over these next three months changes quite quickly. A six-month-old might be having two to three pureed meals a day as well as milk feeds. By nine months, your baby can (messily) feed herself lunch and half of her dinner. The texture of the food is more like a risotto and she is more focused on the fact that she can independently take something to her mouth and know it's food. For parents, it feels like every time they turn around, they're preparing food or feeding the baby! At six to nine months, babies are in a massive growth phase.

There are many theories surrounding babies and food. We hear that French children don't throw food, but that's because they have a different approach to feeding and meal behaviour. In Australia, our tendency is to feed smaller meals more often. Rightly or otherwise, we don't tend to sit down often for meals as a whole family. Outdoor eating is popular, so babies are often fed in the park on summer evenings, for instance. But if we just talk about the development of the babies themselves and what we see, it's no different whether you're sitting in France or here in Australia. At six months, babies everywhere are trying to hold themselves up and their parents have to steady them and feed them; while nine-month-old babies – even the French ones – are all grabbing food and taking it to their mouths.

What does your six-month-old baby need?

A healthy, normally developing six-month-old baby needs two good sleeps in the day and probably a little nap. He needs four milk feeds, two to three meals a day and, generally speaking, he's sleeping through the night or he looks like he's about to. The other sequence would be that he sleeps through the night but twice a week you have to get up to settle him. This is normal.

For parents who might be getting up three times a night to feed their baby, regardless of how he is being fed, there could be a number of things going on. It's not to say anything is wrong, it's just that there might be a point where parents need support to get the baby to sleep better overnight. The most typical thing I see is the baby who was sleeping quite well at night until starting solids. Invariably, parents are unsure about how much to give and when. The baby suddenly starts waking more at night because he's overfed or the feeds are too close to the milk feed. Or the baby's intakes of food are too close and he starts waking for his milk feed.

The transition to solids can be very confusing for parents to negotiate and, again, it's about getting good information. In my chapter on Solids, there are suggestions for food and tips on how to tell when enough's enough!

Babies at six to nine months can be very entertaining and engaging. The relationship between you both is in a good place; your baby smiles at you and turns when he hears a familiar voice. At six months your baby can seek you out.

Physically, a six- to nine-month-old baby is stronger as well. He is no longer always on his back. He is starting to hold a bit of bodyweight and can start to roll and sit up to play. A seven-month-old baby might be able to sit with some cushions around him for support. He will be very interested in his toys and parents have suddenly got a new avenue to entertain the baby by just taking all those toys that are dangling off something, putting them on the floor, making sure the baby is well-supported and then letting him pick them up. Of course, all babies will develop differently, but they generally will sit straight and well somewhere between six and eight months.

By this stage, your baby will have found his voice. Physiologically, his mouth, tongue and jaw are still favouring a sucking motion, but once he is ready for solids, this area strengthens and with the slurping, tongue movement and chewing motion he is developing, so too does his speech.

It is very important to keep offering your child different textures and not rely on packet purees for food. It isn't enough to simply squeeze food into your child's mouth on a regular basis. Despite their convenience (and I'm all for a bit of convenience), these foods are often highly processed with excess water, salt and sugar. It's very easy to make your own food – get a few books from the library for ideas and make your baby food in bulk. See Resources for a few suggestions.

Seven, eight, nine . . . little copycats

By seven months your baby can stay awake a little bit longer during the day. She needs two sleeps a day and she will well and truly be enjoying breakfast, lunch and dinner. She is much more coordinated at getting finger food to her mouth.

A big message for parents at this age is that your baby will be copying everything you do, particularly at meal times. It's important to make the effort to sit down with your baby, even have a little spoonful of mash in a bowl for yourself, to show her that eating is a social event. She will be delighted! You'll notice later when your child goes into day care that she most likely will do very well at eating because they sit in a little group and they watch each other. It's like their own little supper club and it is most likely why she eats chilli con carne at day care and *never* at home!

For a family with a seven-month-old baby that's not sleeping well, it can be very difficult. Being older and bigger, your baby can cry louder and longer. You still need to stay calm and remain consistent. Gentle, simple communication with your baby helps. Offer a little snuggly (soft toy or little blanket) to help your baby go to sleep or rest your hand on her shoulder to calm her, but let her work out how to fall asleep.

Sometimes parents will ask me, 'What if we do nothing to fix the sleeping problem?' My suggestion is that eventually your baby will sleep, but you have to understand that 'eventually' could be three years down the track. It's possible to help babies and children with their sleep patterns at any stage, so if parents find it difficult to address sleep problems at this early age, they needn't if they don't want to. What they *will* need to remember is that eventually, the time will come to help their child and whether it's when she is six months old or three years old, it will require the same two ingredients: patience and consistency. Parents need a lot more support in this phase because babies are louder and they can cry for longer. So even if you're in there patting away, as some people would do, you could be doing it for an hour before your baby responds and goes to sleep. It can be exhausting.

The 6–9 month period is a lot to do with an increasingly engaging baby and growing confidence in parents. Babies smile and 'talk' and put their hands out for you. They laugh and they giggle. You can actually see your baby as a real member of the family. I mean this in a good way. Congratulations, you're doing well!

CHEAT SHEET:
6–9 MONTHS

Note: These are just examples of rhythms and routines for this stage. Babies will generally start their day at around 6–7 am. From there, just work with the rhythm set out below.

6 MONTHS
Awake for periods of 2 hours to 2 hours 30 minutes during the day.

FEEDING

- 4 milk feeds per day

- 1 feed per night or sleeping through

- 2 solids meals

SLEEPING

- 2 sleeps per day in bed – morning 1 hour 30 minutes, afternoon 2 hours

- 1 nap (15–20 minutes)

DEVELOPMENT

- Moving toys from hand to hand or hand to mouth

- Very engaging with newcomers in their life

• A strong love of music

• Rolling and possibly sitting well

SUGGESTED DAILY RHYTHM

6 am milk feed

7 am breakfast

8–9.30 am sleep in bed

10 am milk feed

11.30 am nap

12 pm finger food/lunch

1 pm milk feed

1.30 pm sleep in bed

4.30 pm dinner (veggies)

6.30 pm milk feed and bed routine

7 MONTHS

Awake for periods of 2 hours 30 minutes to 3 hours during the day.

FEEDING

• 4 milk feeds per day

• 3 solids meals

- Finger food

- Food texture should be like mash, if they can handle it

SLEEPING

- 2 sleeps per day in bed – morning 1 hour 30 minutes, afternoon 2 hours to 2 hours 30 minutes

DEVELOPMENT

- Exploring more food with hands

- Sitting up and some will be rocking to a crawl, or crawling quite well

- Generally sleeping through the night more often

SUGGESTED DAILY RHYTHM

6 am milk feed

7 am breakfast

8.30–10 am sleep in bed

10 am milk feed

12 pm lunch

1 pm milk feed

1.30 to 3.30–4.30 pm sleep in bed

5 pm dinner (veggies + protein)

6.30 pm milk feed and bed routine

9 MONTHS

Awake for periods of 3 hours to 3 hours 30 minutes during the day.

FEEDING

• 3 milk feeds per day

• 3 solids meals

• 1 snack

• Food texture should be like risotto

SLEEPING

• 2 sleeps per day in bed – morning 1 hour, afternoon 2–3 hours

DEVELOPMENT

• At around this time, your baby may be crawling – if she is already, she can pull to stand and possibly walk before 12 months.

• The great thing about your 9-month-old's rhythm is that she will generally stay in it until she is around 14–15 months old, when she will move to one sleep per day.

• Very independent with food and will try most finger foods.

SUGGESTED DAILY RHYTHM

6 am milk feed

7 am breakfast

9–10 am sleep in bed

10 am snack

12 pm lunch

1 pm milk feed

1.30 to 3.30–4.30 pm sleep in bed

5 pm dinner (veggies + protein), finger food

6.30 pm milk feed and bed routine

25

9–12 MONTHS + DAY CARE

THE best thing about getting to nine months is that the rhythm of the routine your baby is in will remain this way for another six months or so. For a while now, your baby will enjoy three good meals, three milk feeds, a couple of snacks, two day sleeps and, hopefully, a full night's sleep. Things are pretty predictable. It's also around this time that parents may be thinking of going back to work. There's a feeling of comfort that carers of the baby will follow their pattern of consistency because it's going to be quite a long period of time before there's a need to think about a shift in the baby's daily routine (which will come at around fourteen months when they move to one daytime sleep).

Between nine and twelve months the main thing is that your baby will have lots of physical and cognitive development, such as pulling to stand up and starting to balance on his own feet.

He might begin to crawl with a lot of confidence and start to coordinate movements such as putting objects into spaces and pulling them back out again. In fact, glue down the remote control and hide your wallet – at this age, they are your baby's favourite items to 'post'!

Your baby's fine motor skills are developing rapidly and cognitive thought is flying along. My theory is that your baby's routine and rhythm has to slow down and be really consistent because he is developing in such a rapid way and it takes a lot of physical and mental energy. When babies are learning to crawl, there is a lot of time spent going down a step, up a step, down a step, up a step, pulling up to the coffee table, going down, pulling up, going down. They learn to balance on their feet, so they wobble around for a long time. Your baby can independently feed himself little sandwiches and cut-up pieces of food. It's a time of great exploration!

I often think that the period from nine to about fourteen months is an especially lovely time with a baby. There's predictability, independence and a huge period of growth. Your baby's curiosity is funny and you can see his own little character developing. He is quite an individual and he will also be very sociable (as long as you're within view, usually). Babies this age enjoy being with other babies, but they'll crawl right over the top of them as well. They still like to have parents close; in fact, there's a stage of development that happens around nine months called 'peak of attachment' where the baby is very attached to the primary caregiver. For instance, if the baby's main carer steps out of the room to go to the bathroom, he gets upset. He's trying to learn distance and time. Mum's gone for a minute, then she comes back for a few minutes; then she goes for a few minutes because she's hanging the washing out or whatever she's doing, and then she comes back. It's complex learning for a baby because he's getting to know that mum isn't disappearing forever when she nips out to the loo.

For babies this age, life is very much in the now. If they see something they would like to do, they will go and do it. If it's pulling the cat's tail and the cat has either bolted or been taken away, they will turn their attention to the ball sitting beside them and play with that. They're much more decisive in what they do. They have choice, so they'll choose whether they like some foods and not others.

Temperament and personality start to really come through at this age. The most frequent demonstration is usually at meal times where, if your baby doesn't like the taste or texture of something, she will firmly shut her mouth and turn her head away. It's very distinct. She is no longer trickable! Well, she'll take the trick but she won't eat if she doesn't want to.

By this stage, parents are making decisions on, well, parenting. Things such as parenting style; what matters and how they see family values coming into play. Quite often, parents are also thinking about having another baby. Some swear they will never do it again and others can't wait to add to their family.

Going to day care

I believe that, where at all possible, you should have more hours *with* than away from your child. I can't understand people who think it's fine if a child spends one hour a day with their parent/s. It can't be fine if they're spending ten hours with a carer and one hour with the parent. Okay, they might be physically fine and they will still call their mother and father their parents, but in the long-term, it must have an effect on the child; who they're going to connect with and how they understand the dynamic of their family.

I understand that it is okay to have an opinion like that but I also understand the reality is that some parents have to go back to work full-time. Babies of these parents need to be cared for with a consistent pattern. Some kids will go through a cluttered day where there are multiple people caring for them. Mum and dad might go to work early and grandma comes in for the early morning. Later that morning your baby might be off to day care. In the late afternoon, a nanny might pick her up from day care before mum and dad come home to put her to bed. This could happen one day a week or five days a week for five years before she goes to school.

My message to parents is, again, find the most consistent pattern of as few carers as possible for your child. I suggest to parents that one parent goes to work early while the other does a day care drop-off. The one going to work early does the day care pick-up and the late leaver in the morning has a later finish at the end of the day. What most parents end up doing comes down to affordability and this is sad. I love the Scandinavian model where the government knows how important it is that parents stay at home with their children to the age of two. They support parents to stay at home – usually with mum taking one year off work and dad taking the other. It's about a community recognising what is important for our kids.

Home-based care, in my view, is wonderful because the most familiar thing for your child is her home. If parents need to work, a carer might come in, but it's in the same environment, so it's quite stable for the child, even though people are coming and going. In the end a parent has to do the very best that they can do with what they have. There are always consequences, though. If your child has to go to day care five days a week and you have to drop her off at 7 am and pick her up at 6 pm, then you have to give 110 per cent from 6 am to 7 am, and from 6 pm until 7.30 or whenever she goes to bed. Giving 110 per cent of your focus twice a day is better than no focus all day. But remember, you have to take care of your own relationship as well. The work–life balance is a hard one to master – even more so when you have children. Just be aware that for a baby, one of the ways she will tell you it's not working is through tantrums and challenging behaviour. If she's very young, she may cry a lot.

CHEAT SHEET:
9–12 MONTHS

WHAT TO EXPECT

Awake periods of 3 hours to 3 hours 30 minutes during the day, with generally only two sleeps per day in bed

- Morning 1 hour

- Afternoon 2–3 hours

This is a very predictable period of development. These routines usually stay much the same to about 14 months at which point many babies move to one sleep period per day.

During this stage, a baby's fine and gross motor skills develop a lot. They enjoy eating and trying to eat independently using hands. Many babies are crawling, pulling to stand, walking, eating finger food and picking up things with their fingertips.

It is a very busy time and a good idea to review the danger zones in and around your home.

9 MONTHS

Sleep needs are about 3 hours to 3 hours 30 minutes per day.

FEEDING

- 3 meals

- 1 snack

- 3 milk feeds

- Drinking water from a cup

SUGGESTED DAILY RHYTHM

6–7 am feed (9–14 months)

Breakfast

9–10 am sleep in bed

Snack

12 pm lunch

1 pm feed

1.30 to 3.30–4 pm sleep in bed

5 pm dinner

6 pm bath

6.30 pm feed

7-ish bed

12 MONTHS

Sleep needs are about 2 hours 30 minutes to 3 hours per day.

FEEDING

- 3 meals

- 2–3 milk feeds

- 1–2 snacks

- Drinking water from a cup

A daily rhythm for babies at this age is very similar to a 9-month-old except that some babies will only sleep for about 40 minutes in the morning and have a long afternoon sleep.

Babies will often move to cow milk if on formula.

Offer milk, formula, expressed breast milk or water in a sippy cup.

26

12–18 MONTHS

YOUR child at twelve to eighteen months old is becoming an independent little eater, thinker and, perhaps, talker!

Her growing independence is delightfully obvious at this stage. She will be developing her own sense of belonging within your family and she will enjoy meal times, playing with you and generally being part of the family. She knows she belongs and this is lovely.

Language development is also a huge part of this age. By the time she is eighteen months old, your child will have a good grasp of very simple language such as 'no', 'yes', 'mummy' and 'daddy'. If she is asked a direct question she is able to understand, she will answer just as directly! She can process a cognitive thought and give very basic language responses.

In terms of your rhythm and routine, your child will be steadily moving to one sleep during the day. It happens somewhere in the window between fourteen and fifteen months. You'll know when to tweak it when one of the two sleeps your child is currently having gets shorter. For instance, if she is sleeping for an hour in the morning and two hours in the afternoon, she might start sleeping for half an hour in the morning and an hour in the afternoon and then being really whingey by the end of the day. If you start to merge those two sleeps together, your child would be much more tolerant in the day because she's well-rested and will go to bed easier at night. Some children won't actually change their daytime sleep pattern and they'll still go to sleep easily at seven o'clock at night. The problem here is that they start waking at five in the morning where they used to be sleeping until six or seven. It's a case of your child saying to you, 'I just don't need as much sleep.'

By combining the sleeps in the day, you end up getting back to a consistent pattern of sleep. Some children keep slumbering away twice a day until they're almost fifteen or sixteen months old, and still sleep well at night. So it's quite loose as to when you do it, but if you aim for around fourteen months, generally it will work. That sleep will then slowly push out over fourteen, sixteen and eighteen months. So you might start putting your child into bed at 11.30 am and letting her sleep for two to two and a half hours. After a few months, you notice she is not tired at 11.30 am, so you wait until noon for a sleep. Eventually, at eighteen months she is going to bed at 12.30 pm and will sleep until 2.30 pm. After this sleep, most children can happily stay awake for about five hours. This gets your child to about 7.30 pm when she should be able to sleep quite well throughout the night.

This sleep pattern continues until your child is about three, give or take windows of time. I wouldn't suggest it stops earlier than two and a half or you will be faced with daily tantrums from an overtired child. Likewise, a child who is three and a half years old having a two-hour sleep in the afternoon might be tricky to get to bed before 9 pm. It's a matter of adjusting the time you put your child into bed, taking into account the length of time she can happily stay awake for afterwards, and the time you want her to go to sleep.

Physically, your child is becoming a lot more coordinated. She could start walking at any point from now on. The earliest you tend to see babies walk is around ten months and the latest you'd want them to start walking is around eighteen months. Any later than this means you should probably have a think about what's going on developmentally. It might mean a bit of physiotherapy if your child has low muscle tone or it might simply mean you need to stop carrying your child around and give her the chance to walk!

Meal times will be incredibly messy but you need to let them happen. Your burgeoning toddler can feed himself quite consistently, either by hand, spoon or fork. Try to encourage drinking out of an open cup, even though this can get *extremely* messy. (Go to the two-dollar shop and get a bright shower curtain and put it under the high chair = problem solved.)

A message for parents: Sometimes we have to work out why your child is not doing things. And occasionally it's because parents aren't giving them the opportunity to do it. Like drinking out of a cup. I know it's messy but if you pour a small amount in, what's the worst that can happen? A small spillage, and yet your child has learned to drink from a cup. If you have a three-year-old drinking out of a bottle, think about this!

By eighteen months children can truly get across what they need, either verbally or physically. I love this period. It's funny and the babies think they're born geniuses because they stand up and they look around as if to say, 'I have stood up and I'm the only person in the whole world who has ever done it!'. Having said that, eighteen-month-old children have very little concept of space – or danger, for that matter. There are usually a few bruises from tumbles but they're pretty sturdy, really. Let your child explore but stay close. They can be fast, so in crowds, near cars and especially near water – keep an eye on them at all times. Now is a good time to childproof your house – in fact, this is a good weekend job. Your local hardware shop will have everything you need.

More than anything, you have to have time and patience. Take your child to the park and let her have a really good wander about. Pick up leaves. Play in the dirt. Chase the birds. Try not to hover, apart from keeping her safe. When you're at home, let your child unload the bottom drawer in the kitchen. What a discovery! Unload the tissue box and then shove it all back in again. Brilliant! Children love nothing more than a good unravelling of the toilet roll – let her do it.

Tantrums

Fast-growing children of this age can get extremely frustrated when they can't either physically or mentally communicate their needs. If your child is getting enough good sleep and she's throwing the odd tantrum, I'm willing to bet she's frustrated about something – usually to do with play. Be patient, wait until the tantrum stops and then help her solve the problem. Without hovering too close, you can usually pre-empt a tantrum but make sure you let your child think she has solved it first.

Children need time to calm down from a tantrum. Keep yours safe but remain disengaged. There is little you can do to explain a complex square-peg-round-hole issue to an eighteen-month-old when she's upset and frustrated. Keep calm and things will settle. Use simple words in a gentle voice such as, 'You need to calm down now.' Fixing the issue for them or disciplining at this age is futile. Give your child a cuddle and say, 'Come on then, let's go and put the square peg in the square hole; mummy (or daddy) will show you how to do it.'

If you feel your child is constantly having tantrums, you need to see if there is something else going on. It's usually one of three things: tiredness, lack of attention from parents, or rushing. Which brings me back to the basics of looking at what your child needs.

CHEAT SHEET:
12–18 MONTHS

14 MONTHS
FEEDING

- 2 milk feeds

- 1–2 snacks

- 3 meals

- Drinking water from a cup

1 daytime sleep for 2–3 hours.

Feeding himself.

Offer milk in a cup with meals.

Offer water when needed.

SUGGESTED DAILY RHYTHM

6 am (or on waking) feed

Breakfast

11 am lunch

11.30 am to 2–2.30 pm sleep in bed

2.30 pm (or on waking) snack

5 pm dinner

6 pm bath

6.30 pm feed

7-ish pm bed

16 MONTHS

FEEDING

• 1 milk feed

• 1-2 snacks

• 3 meals

• Introduce spoon and fork

1 daytime sleep for 2 hours to 2 hours 30 minutes.

SUGGESTED DAILY RHYTHM

On waking – breakfast

9 am morning tea

11.30 am lunch

12–2.30 pm sleep in bed

2.30 pm (or on waking) snack

5 pm dinner

6 pm bath

6.30 pm feed

7-ish pm bed

18 MONTHS

FEEDING

• No more milk feeds required, but may be debated between child and parent

• 2 snacks

• 3 meals

1 daytime sleep for 2 hours 30 minutes – this may continue until 2½–3½ years.

Can take milk in a cup – may drink independently from a cup.

Move babies off bottles.

SUGGESTED DAILY RHYTHM

On waking – breakfast

9–9.30 am morning tea

12 pm lunch

12.30–2 pm sleep in bed

2 pm (or on waking) snack

5 pm dinner

6 pm bath

6.30 pm milk in cup (and perhaps a story before bed)

7-ish pm bed

27

TODDLERS

TODDLERS are an institution unto themselves. I'm convinced they think they are the leaders of the free world. You will have days when one minute you're wondering how something so small can create so much chaos and the next minute smile so beautifully, you melt. There is so much going on for the toddler *and* for you. It's an incredibly busy time with lots of change so hang on for the ride! Looking after yourself is very important during this stage and if you've got other children, you and your partner will need to keep working on communicating and sharing the load.

Some of the major changes that will take place in your toddler's life include changing from his cot to a 'big' bed, toilet training and perhaps going to day care, if he isn't there already. There is also a lot of development with language, sleep, feeding and socialisation. Like all children, toddlers mature physically, mentally and emotionally at different times so don't compare your child with others. Everything seems to intertwine at this stage. One day your toddler will be doing something beautiful, delightful and gorgeous and the next he will be the household warrior.

Toddlers are unintentionally, incredibly self-centred. It will seem as if he has the shortest temper of anyone you know but the reality is there is a lot of frustration at this age. Be patient and be prepared to slow down while he works things out – with your help.

Probably the most important thing to know about toddlers is that with increased curiosity and energy comes tiredness. It might look as if your toddler has endless energy and he can just 'go, go, go' but if you let him, he will get overtired. They voice their frustration and fatigue through tantrums and, being a bit bigger and stronger and louder, those tantrums can go on and on . . .

Choices, choices . . .

Toddlers also want to do everything (for) themselves. Allow me a friendly word about *choice* here. I know you want to foster independence in your child, but you don't often have all day to do it, so give your toddler choices only when you have the *time* to see it through. Don't give him a choice if you're trying to get out the door in five minutes. It's a really important thing for parents with toddlers to understand. You need *time* and *patience* to allow your child to sort through his options to work it out himself. If you haven't got the time, it's okay to say, 'Actually, we're going to do X today.'

Sometimes you have to stop and sit back to think about the world that your toddler lives in. Occasionally your child might have a day at home in his own little world, happy in the kitchen unloading the Tupperware drawer. But mostly it's all a bit of a rush. When this happens to your toddler, he feels incredibly disorganised and it's up to you to organise him. You need to organise his feelings; you need to be bigger and wiser and to be his leader. If you're flat-out all the time and you're battling tantrums, try a few days at home to quieten things down and see what happens. You won't regret it, I'm sure.

Food and your toddler

Your eighteen-month-old should be enjoying family food at meal times and should be able to drink out of a cup by now. Between nine and eighteen months, your toddler will eat well – in fact, he'll probably eat anything that's going past him. This is a good thing because as toddlers move towards age three, they become quite particular about food, often only eating three-quarters of familiar foods and resisting new foods altogether. Don't fight it.

I see many parents who worry about meal times and food. Yet I think it's one thing you shouldn't argue about with your toddler. If you're struggling to get your child to eat, think about *when* he's eating and *what*. Are your meal times regular? Are portion sizes reasonable? Is the food reasonable? How much has your child had to eat over the course of the day? Toddlers quite like individual portions of food. They like to see the peas, the sausage, the potato, and they want to pick up the food with their fingers. The more you use your knife and fork in front of them, the more they will want to.

Portion size is important too. A meal the size of an adult's palm, or one that covers the area of the base of a toddler bowl, is actually quite a generous portion. Many parents make the mistake of feeding children more than they want when it's better to give them a smaller amount and if they eat it, then you can always give them some more. If you give a toddler a large plate of food all (beautifully) intertwined, they will likely test all theories (and your patience) and give it a good fling across the room. It's because that bowl full of food is overwhelming. If you took that same bowl and put in two chips, a few peas and a couple of bits of sausage, your toddler is more likely to look at an uncluttered bowl of food and eat what's in it. Similarly, if your toddler is eating well at day care and refusing food at home, don't worry; eating at day care is a social activity and children eat because everyone else is!

I've mentioned that in Australia, we tend to feed our children more regularly than the three standard meals a day. This can have its issues because toddlers often aren't getting three meals and two snacks, they're getting five small meals. If your toddler is going to day care, there's a fair chance he will be offered something to eat late in the afternoon. He is unlikely to want to eat dinner an hour after he has eaten afternoon tea so, on day care days, offer your child something very simple for dinner – cheese or avocado on toast, or a boiled egg with toast soldiers is completely fine.

Table etiquette and eating out

Since eating is a social activity, it stands to reason you should be setting examples on how to behave socially at meal times. Thankfully, we've come a long way from 'You're not getting dessert until you've finished your vegetables' and the old 'Don't speak until you're spoken to'. It's fun to have kids at the table and you should all be able to enjoy meal times together. If you struggle to sit down together for a meal during the week, make a ritual of eating together at the weekend. As your children grow up, they will know that meal times are a place where the family comes together to enjoy food *and* conversation. Put the electronics away and teach your toddler how to ask questions and listen to the answers. Give everyone a turn to speak and tell your toddler you like hearing about what they did that day. Sometimes you will take ages to finish your dinner but I bet you'll hear something from your child that will make you laugh until you cry. Some of my funniest moments have been with toddlers at meal times.

> Tip: Toddlers can only sit for about twenty minutes. If they've eaten reasonably and you're still enjoying the company of some adults, I think it's reasonable for your child to leave the table, have a little play and then come back to have dessert with you.

If you have given your child a reasonable portion of *reasonable* food, it is therefore reasonable for you to expect your child to try it. You should resist making sausages for one child and fish fingers for another. Instead, offer everyone the same thing and over the course of a few days to a week, make sure what you're offering is balanced enough so you can introduce new foods when you think they're ready. If you offer new food with things you know they like, you can say, 'I can't make you like it, but I would like you to try it.' If your child doesn't taste it, don't then offer her a yoghurt (or whatever her preferred food is) straight afterwards to fill her up.

By the time your toddler is about three, she will start to experiment more with food. She is used to sitting at the table with you and with her friends at day care and she is understanding that what she is offered for a meal isn't likely to be horrible! You could happily go out for dinner but just make sure the restaurant is kid-friendly if possible. Order simple things for your toddler and offer some of your food as a taster.

Processing and predictability

Toddlers need processing time. If you're ready to go out and your child is in the middle of a major unloading of the Tupperware drawer and you whisk her up, saying, 'We're going down the street now', chances are she will have a tantrum. Five minutes before you want to leave, you're better off saying, 'It's time to pack up because we're going to hop in the car and go to the shops.' If you watch teachers at day cares and preschools, they do this constantly. They're always telling the children when something's going to finish and when something's going to start. 'We're going to pack up now. It's pack-up time.' You know it's working when your toddler comes home and you say, 'We're going to have dinner in five minutes', and they say, 'Oh, it's pack-up time.' If you need to get things moving a bit quicker, ask nicely, wait for it to sink in, go over to your toddler, maybe start the job and ask them to help. Remember, your toddler is only young and sometimes she just needs to be stirred from her 'work'.

Fitting in with a new arrival

Helping your toddler adjust to having a baby sibling can be challenging. It's easy to forget that the toddler is a toddler and will have tantrums because she *is* a toddler, not because you have a new baby.

I think the biggest mistake that parents make with their toddler when a sibling arrives is that nobody changes what's happening with the toddler. The toddler's world stays the same but all this chaos is going on around her. Despite their determination to do things their own way, toddlers can actually be very pliable! What you have to remember is that the changes you make need to be as devoid of chaos as possible. Try to keep the toddler's basic rhythm of their day the same. It's important that they see the people who are familiar in their week-to-week or day-to-day life. If they normally go to day care, they should go to day care. If mum's in hospital and grandma has arrived from afar to help, then dad needs to be at home to put the toddler to bed, not grandma. Remember, your toddler really won't know a distant relative who has turned up two days prior to mum going into hospital to have this baby that everyone's been talking about. For your toddler, *this is chaotic.*

For the parents of a newborn and toddler, this can be a very intense time. The new baby zaps all your physical strength and the toddler's zapping all your mental strength, so you're pretty shattered by the time the baby's six months old. The best way to parent your toddler is to keep that predictability going for them, just keep it swinging along, tick, tick, tick. You will need to make changes to your toddler's routine but try to make as few as possible in the six weeks before and after the baby arrives. Just keep it as predictable as possible and try not to make consolations for the toddler, such as putting her to bed later because you need time to feed the baby. Your toddler just needs to go to bed when she should go to bed. If she is not getting what she needs, she is likely to let you know in the form of a tantrum.

When you do need to make a few changes to your toddler's day, go back to basics and think about what she needs. Now is a great time for dad to take her to the park, or do the day care drop-off and pick-up, if he isn't doing it already. Make the changes slowly and with lots of conversation. You're just giving your child what she needs, which is time and patience to process the change. In the long run, this works out better for you all.

Sleep and settling

After enjoying a good nine to twelve months of a familiar day/night pattern, your toddler's sleep pattern is likely to change. If she is still having long sleeps in the day, she could be difficult to get to sleep at night. The first thing I would do is look at how much sleep she is having. Too much or too little during the day can make nights tricky.

I have a theory that toddlers should be up from their daytime sleep between 2 and 2.30 pm regardless of how much sleep they've had beforehand. Between eighteen months and, say, two and a half years, children need somewhere between an hour and a half to two hours sleep during the day to be rested enough. But here's the thing: they need to be up at 2–2.30 pm in order to go to bed happily in the evening. So if your little toddler sleeps until 3 pm, still goes to bed at 7 or 7.30 pm quite happily and then wakes at 6–6.30 am, her sleep pattern is working well. If your toddler is having two and a half hours sleep and getting up at 3 pm, finding it more difficult to go to bed at 7.30 pm and then waking at 5 am, you should consider starting to reduce her day sleep. The more you can control it, the longer she'll keep it. If you reduce the day sleep down by half an hour and wake her at 2.30 pm, she's going to be happier to go to bed at 7.30 pm. Keeping this bedtime will enable her to have a better night's sleep through until whenever she wakes in the morning.

How do you know when your toddler is ready to give up her daytime sleep?

The most obvious way to tell if your toddler is ready to give up her daytime sleep is that she is increasingly tricky to settle at night. You put her into bed at 7.30 pm and the circus begins. She needs to go to the toilet, or perhaps she needs to squeeze in another hug, maybe a drink of water, another story, a back tickle, a side tickle, not enough tickles, too much tickling . . . and on it goes.

The first thing you need to do is check how much sleep is going on during the day. When your toddler is down to about an hour's sleep, usually when she reaches age two to two and a half, and she's sleeping through the night, start to bring her nap time down to about twenty minutes. You might do this by encouraging her to snuggle under a little blanket on the couch while she watches a (low-excitement level) show on the television. You might put her in the car at 12.30 pm and go for a drive while she naps until one o'clock. It's enough to keep the temperament of your toddler more stable for the rest of the day, but it's not so much so that she won't go to sleep at night.

Bedtime shenanigans

Once you have the daytime nap reducing, you need to stop the bedtime circus, if it isn't decreasing already. As the parent, it's okay to say, 'Actually, you're going to bed', and once you make that shift and change, your child will respond. All you need to do is make sure you've met all your child's needs, such as a reasonable rest in the day so she's not overtired, or some quiet time if she no longer needs a sleep. Your bedtime rhythm should only take about twenty minutes, including teeth cleaning, loo stop, bedtime story and a little chat about the day. This doesn't take an hour and a half. Remember, it's not about your child being *asleep* at 7.30 pm, it's actually just about them being quiet and restful because that's half the process of going to bed. If the circus begins, just go to the door and quietly say, 'It's time for sleep.' Don't engage in conversation and general chitchat. Be firm, stand quietly at the door if you have to, but stick to your guns. It's bedtime!

Nightmares and night terrors

The difference between a nightmare and night terrors is that when your child has a night terror she won't respond to your comfort. It's as if she's in a sleep state, but she's crying and telling you that there is a monster in the cupboard. When you try to comfort her, she will continue thrashing around and won't let you hold her. It can be very upsetting but try not to worry. The best thing to do is make sure she can't hurt herself and quietly let her work herself through it. Night terrors usually happen in the same two-hour window at night. There's not a lot you can do as she won't remember anything about it the next morning. She'll grow out of it.

Nightmares are different. Your child will be quite awake, alert, and she will want comfort from you. She will be happy for you to pick her up and give her a cuddle and she'll tell you about the monster in the cupboard. You can 'take the monster outside and tell it to never come back again' and she will (hopefully) be relieved to see it 'gone'. You might have to help your toddler to settle back to sleep and be firm about her staying in bed, but don't worry too much – it will pass.

Little geniuses

I love the way toddlers discover something new every day and think that they are the ones that invented it. It's hilarious. Boys learn to do that funny skip and they think they're brilliant. Even though they are completely uncoordinated at it, they think they're so clever. So you just clap hands and tell them it's fantastic. Away they go! A toddler's 'work' *is* to work things out. One day they can't have a conversation and the next day they're in charge of everyone. I just love the fact that toddlers think they're the only person that's ever walked or stuck their finger up your nose. Taps are fascinating and the whole toilet thing is endless fodder for fun. Isn't exploration and discovery the essence of a human being? And you've got it happening right in front of you.

By the time toddlers turn three they're all doing pretty much the same thing. Look at your day care centres and preschools. They don't split activities into boy and girl focus. Everyone is doing the same thing. But get them outside and you can see the gentle divide. Preferences for doing one thing over another will start to come out and this will change constantly over the course of their lives.

Parenting toddlers

One of the many interesting things I talk about with parents of toddlers is the way their own parents raised them. There's a lot of consideration given to this and it's a time when parents are thinking about how they want their children to be brought up. I always remind them that when you come from differing backgrounds, there will be an amount of conflict. The important thing is that you both have a say on what you would like to see in your child. The work is in resolving your differences to find a technique that will incorporate your family values.

One of you might have been brought up to sit at the table at meal times until everybody's finished, while the other might have never experienced this at all. Working out who you are as a family and living those family values is what matters. You can start with what you fundamentally want and then ask yourselves what is reasonable for your child.

As parents, you need more skills to navigate through this than you did when you first had a newborn. Now that your child is getting older, there's a whole raft of things that are on a social, emotional and psychological level in terms of your child's development. Couples will have differences, but the secret to success is in communicating what you feel and putting your child's *needs* into the picture. If you can't resolve your differences, there are many ways to get help. See Resources for a few suggestions.

So the golden rule with toddlers is to give them time. Sit back and laugh with them, lie on the trampoline and discuss what shape the clouds are. A toddler's a toddler, and toddlers need your guidance and support, your patience and, most of all, you.

28

TOILET TRAINING

W ITH different customs and family values, there's a lot to be said about toilet training, but there are a couple of fundamental things that you must have in place before a child's going to be able to toilet train. The first is that your child needs to be able to communicate with you. He needs to be able to say, 'I need to go to the toilet.' You know they're fully toilet trained when you can say, 'You need to hang on for five minutes, we'll be home and then you can go to the toilet', and your child *will*!

The second is the ability to know when they should go, not when they're about to go!

Timing v training

Toilet training is about the maturity of the child and over time we've realised that, generally speaking, girls do it much faster than boys and, generally speaking again, they tend to do it better around the age of two and a half. When people tell me that they can hold out their nine-month-old and she'll be toilet trained, I suggest they are not toilet *training*, they are toilet *timing*. There is a difference. Toilet *training* is the ability for the child to independently take themselves to the toilet. Toilet *timing* is where the child may be wearing underwear, but the parent is guiding the child to toiletting by saying things like, 'Come on, we need to go to the toilet now', and they put her on the toilet at regular intervals. That's toilet timing and children toilet *time* before they toilet *train*.

If you start too early because all the mothers in your mothers' group think it's a good idea and little Johnny (one in seven) did it and he's fantastic, then you're putting a lot of pressure on yourself. Often you can start too early and you're still doing it six months later, whereas if you'd just waited the six months you could probably do it in two weeks.

The first sign that your child is ready for toilet training is that he will tell you that he has 'done' something and will often hold his nappy. He is also keen to sit on the toilet! That's because they're seeing everybody in their community doing it. They're walking in when mum and dad are on the loo (sorry, but it's true) and they're seeing the 'big' kids at day care go to the toilet. It's going on all around him so he is keen to get in on the fun.

Your eighteen-month-old is usually not interested, although he will go over to the toilet and drop something in there (hilarious). It could be your keys, it could be your phone, it could be that he just wants to push the button all the time. But children about two years old actually see the sequence.

They stand, they take their underwear down, they do a wee, they flush the toilet (hopefully), they wash and dry their hands, and then they move on. But I still think at age two they don't have the maturity to actually link the bit about recognising the feeling of needing to do a wee, stopping what they're doing and allowing enough time to get to the loo and get on it!

As for most things to do with children, there is no hard and fast rule about when everything is going to happen. It's very hard on parents when organisations like childcare centres won't advance children to their age-level classroom if they are not toilet trained. That's an incredible pressure to put on a parent of a child who may not be ready to toilet train; it's ridiculous, I think. In some cases, there are childcare centres who will not take children at all unless they are toilet trained. Crazy.

The other signs your child is ready for toilet training include telling you his nappy is wet or trying to take his nappy off because he dislikes the feeling of it being wet. Some parents get terribly excited when their child has announced that he's done a poo in his nappy. This is great, but it means he's ready to be taught to do it on the loo.

At around two and a half years, it all starts to come together. Your child is communicating well, he's not weeing in his nappy as much and his bowels are becoming quite regular. It's easier for parents to initiate the concept of toilet training. Even when children are fully toilet trained during the day, it can take another six months to a year for them to be dry at night. So the idea is not to put pressure on your child. If he doesn't make it to the toilet in time, don't worry. Just be supportive and say, 'Woops, I think we need to stop playing a bit sooner next time.'

Once your child is in underpants, remain consistent. You can't turn around after all that effort and say, 'We're trying to toilet train you but now we're going on a three-hour car ride so we'll put a nappy on you', because that's demoralising to the child, especially if he's holding on and you're telling him to wee in his nappy while you're driving along.

Summer, providing the age timing works, is a good time to toilet train. Clothing and bedding is lighter, the days are warm, and if there are misfires and badly timed trips to the toilet, the washing isn't a huge issue. Put two plastic-backed, towelling sheet protectors (see Resources for suggestions on where to buy these) on your child's bed so if he wets the bed and wakes in the night, you can take the wet one off, quickly change your child and everyone's back to bed and sleep without fuss.

Working out when to 'go'

I know there are a lot of different methods out there, but let's look at a reasonable approach. If you rush your child to the toilet every twenty minutes, all she'll do is a little wee. She's not emptying her bladder. Twenty minutes later, the same thing happens and before long you have a worried child who thinks she's disappointing her parents because nothing's coming out! The better approach is to wait until your child has a good grasp of language, that she's roughly around two and a half, and she is interested in people going to the toilet. I'm not a huge fan of potties – I figure you might as well just use the toilet with a soft seat insert and a little step.

Recognising what her body feels like before she needs to go to the toilet is a learned thing, so for about a week you will need to toilet *time* your child. Again, this is where you initiate taking your child to the toilet by using very simple language and saying things like, 'We are going to the toilet now to try and do a wee before we go to the park', or 'Let's go and try to do a wee before bed'. I suggest you do this about four or five times a day; mid morning, lunch time, mid afternoon, maybe around bath or bedtime. At this stage, your child will still be wearing a nappy or pull-up. What you're looking for over the week is getting two or three wees in the toilet during the day. A week later, if you've got a child that's looking at the ceiling and discussing the mould across your bathroom, they're no more interested in toilet training than flying to the moon – I'd probably suggest you stop, wait a month and then start the whole thing again. Don't keep going and pushing your child. She's not interested; she's not ready.

Toilet timing is a little tester to see where your child is at: will she follow a suggestion to go to the toilet? Make sure you've set the toilet up in a way that's reasonable for your child and don't worry too much about poos at this stage. Many children will want to use a nappy to do a poo – oddly enough they can sometimes feel like they're losing a part of their body so the nappy gives them a sense of security.

Once you've had a pretty successful week doing toilet timing, you can start the second week by taking off your child's day nappy (because she will use night nappies for much longer), giving her bottom a little freshen up with a cloth or baby wipe and popping a little pair of underpants on her. Try not to go too far from a toilet this week; it might be to your local park and back – but not on a three-hour outing, which is a completely unrealistic expectation and you're only setting yourselves up to go backwards. Tell your child that the toilet's all set up with her step at home and that she needs to tell you when she needs to go to the toilet.

The first day usually sees your child telling you she's doing a wee on the floor because she hasn't yet worked out how long it takes to get from the kitchen to the bathroom. It's a little 'accident' – no problem. Wipe your child down, pop some clean underwear on her and off you go. Remind her to tell you when she needs to go to the toilet. As the day goes on, you will inevitably spot your child doing the 'wee-wee dance' where she stands in one spot and jumps up and down – cue the loo. By about the second and third day, your child is actually making it onto the toilet, possibly yelling to you as she's running to the bathroom, 'I need to do a wee-wee.' As she gets to the toilet, give her a little helping hand. As the week goes on, she might make it to the toilet regularly but you need to keep offering gentle reminders to go before you go out, before bed and so on.

Don't nag!

Children tend to go to the toilet two or three times over the course of a day, maybe more in summer if they're drinking more water. If you keep asking your child on the hour if he needs to go to the toilet, he will switch off to your language. If you're heading out to the park and you ask your child if he needs to go to the toilet and he says no, just say okay, and put a spare pair of undies into a plastic bag along with a couple of wipes. You will soon get to know how long your child can go between trips to the loo. If (when) you're at the park and he needs to go (Murphy's Law will activate and it's almost certain to happen), and then he has a little 'accident', clean up as usual and press on. Next time you go out and you suggest a trip to the loo before leaving, he will probably remember the last trip and realise that what you're suggesting is a good idea!

As the days progress, your child now understands how to get his body to do a wee, what his body feels like when he needs to do a wee or a poo, and he understands timing. He is able to think, 'I'm up on the slide and I need to go to the toilet. I need to get down off the slide and the toilet seems to be over there' – so he will stop what he's doing and make a conscious decision to get to the toilet in time.

Bribery and corruption – don't do it

We all use a bit of bribery and corruption for occasional things but don't do it with toilet training. If you bribe your child with a chocolate every time you want her to go to the toilet – or worse, you reward her with sweets every time she goes – you're going to need a good dentist. This is an everyday thing so keep it business-as-usual. After a successful trip to the loo, have a quick clapping of hands and say, 'Good girl, let's wash our hands and let's go!'. No fuss, no bother. Save your bribes for important occasions like a lengthy wait at the doctor's surgery.

28

COT TO BED

GENERALLY speaking, around the same time that your child has the cognitive development to toilet train, she's usually got the cognitive development to go into a bed. Lots of people move their children into beds for lots of different reasons. Some schools of thought argue that toddlers should go into a bed at fifteen months but I disagree. The idea behind using toilet training as a marker is that a child has to independently make a choice to go to the toilet, wash her hands and so on. She needs guidance and lots of time to learn. Going to a 'big' bed is the same. Your child will need to have the independent ability to make the choice to stay in bed once you've said goodnight. The most common reason why parents have difficulty transitioning their child from a cot to a bed is because they do it too early. Remember, having another baby is not a reason to move your eighteen-month-old to a cot. It's simply too soon.

Before you decide to make the big move, make sure your child is showing a bit of self control – she will need it to be able to stay in the bed. You should also be confident that your child has an awareness of consequences. This kind of cognitive behaviour happens around the age of two and a half. That said, you could have a two-year-old who is ready, you could have a three-year-old still roaming the halls, and you could have a six-year-old still wandering into your room in the middle of the night. Whenever you decide to make the move, the best way is to do it properly.

Before getting the new bed, set up the cot like a bed. Get a child's pillow, sheets and blankets and make the cot as a bed together. This gives your child the sense of security of her cot but with it made up just like a big bed. Take away the sleeping bag and get some nice new pyjamas for the occasion. Use the cot as a bed for about a week and then, lo and behold, when Saturday comes, the lovely man from the bedding store will arrive with a nice new big bed!

When the new bed arrives, dismantle the cot, but see if you can slide the cot mattress under the bed. If not, just put it aside for now. For the first couple of nights, put it beside the bed so if your child rolls off her bed she'll have a soft landing. Surprisingly, not many kids fall out of bed.

As far as the bedtime routine goes, you don't need to change anything – in fact, it's better if you don't. Just take your child to bed, read a bedtime story, give her a kiss and a cuddle and put her into bed. Don't even mention staying in it, just kiss her goodnight and walk out. If the timing is right, the majority of kids will actually stay there, but a few will get up and walk out.

If this happens with your child, don't engage with her too much on that first night. Just say, 'It's time for bed', and walk her back to bed. You might have to do this three times, six times, twenty-six times, but the message is, 'You're going back to bed, you're going back to bed, you're going back to bed'. It's a dull exercise for you and pretty soon it will be a dull exercise for your child – that's the point. No fun in getting out of bed, I might as well stay there.

When the wandering starts . . .

Sometimes kids happily move into a bed and things go well for around six months and then they start getting the wanders. The second time they do it (usually on a consecutive night), it's time to implement a little consequence. Remember, this is not 'naughty'. A gentle consequence is to get the portacot out and set it up in the middle of the room. It's a little bit small and a little bit uncomfortable for anyone other than a baby. You can then say to your child, 'If you get off the bed I'll have to put you back in the baby cot.' So, if your child gets out of bed, you put her in the portacot, say, 'It's time for sleep', and walk away.

If you don't have a portable cot, take out of the room all the things that your child could climb on. Put a gate across the door and say, 'If you get out of bed, I'm not coming back to put you back in.' At this point, she will most likely come to the gate and cry until she goes to sleep either at the gate or back in her bed. Some people shut the door for this as well. If you are really struggling and your child is continually getting out of bed, then you have to set up the cot again and put your child back in it. It isn't fair for your child to persist with consequences that make no sense, because your child is not being 'naughty', she's just not ready to go into a big bed.

Remember, this isn't about you, it's about your child. If you're happy for the child to come out and sit with you for three hours and then go to bed, or maybe even come into your bed at night, fantastic, keep going with it. But don't say to the child, 'I'm going to get angry because you're not doing what I want you to do', without giving a consequence *that's reasonable for the child*.

If you don't believe in allowing your child to cry at night and you want to have her with you in bed, be happy; buy a king-sized bed. But you can't then say, 'All she wants is me and I've been giving her me for six months and now I don't want to; but I don't want to do anything that's hard work or that upsets my child.' So, yes, you can sit on the floor and wait for your child to go to sleep but in the end she has to lie down in her bed, she has to shut her eyes and she has to go to sleep because that's how you go to sleep. If you don't set up the cot to bed transition properly from the beginning and there's movement and negotiation, then the negotiation will just get bigger and louder as your child gets older.

When your child stays in her bed for the night, make sure you tell her she did a good job and you're proud of her.

30

THOUGHTS ON DISCIPLINE

WHEN I was young, I reckon I lived in a bit of a bubble. The world seemed a much safer place compared with what kids have to deal with now. Maybe it's childhood naivety, but life seemed a lot simpler back in the 1970s! Today, life for children can be chaotic. There could be a number of reasons for this but the pressure placed on parents (either self-imposed or societal) is pretty relentless. Despite these pressures, we rely on kids' ability to adapt and, mostly, we muddle through. This is great, and kids will adapt well if they are given the time to learn and grow, but they still need consistency. Without it, the chaos takes over and family life takes on a wild and unpredictable ride.

For children in 'busy' households – and by this I mean a full day; up early and home late with a packed day of learning and play in between – discipline and learning is often up to a

number of adults. We have a parent or parents, nannies, babysitters, teachers, childcare workers, grandparents – sometimes it's
a long list – all caring for your child. However long the list is,
the most important thing I can say about child discipline and
learning is that *consistency is key*.

When children are very young (but beyond the earliest
baby stage), they rely on repetition. Meal times are a great
example. The baby goes into the high chair, is offered food,
given a spoon, showed how to use the spoon, is fed (or attempts
to do so himself) over and over, at least three times a day, every
day. As your baby gets a little bit older and stretches a bit of
personality muscle, there might be food throwing, reluctance
to get into the high chair or to eat, and so on. This is where
consistency and calmness steps in. You can't force your child to
eat, nor do you want to try explaining the benefits of nutri-
tious food to a two-year-old, so you will need to deal with it
in a way that your child will understand. You might quietly
remove your child from what it is that's creating the problem
or simply take the plate away and put the food in the fridge
for later. You are giving your child the message that unruly
behaviour isn't okay at the table. You keep your child in your
sight and you move on. As your child gets a bit older, you
might remove him, have a little chat about what has happened
and perhaps implement a consequence. This gives your child
the opportunity to make choices, should he be thinking about
a repeat performance at the next meal time.

Thinking about discipline and behaviour is part of
parenting – there's no getting around it.

There is a lot to think about when you choose how to deal
with behaviour or how to discipline your child and there are

many factors that influence your decisions. It can be confusing when you consider the ways that you were raised by (often) two sets of parents, as well as social and cultural trends within your community.

For a young child to be disciplined effectively, he needs to be able to understand what he has done wrong. For most children, understanding this concept happens at around the age of three. You will be able to see in your child's eyes if he knows that what he has done is not okay – in some children it may be at a younger age. You will start to see temperament, behaviours and frustration as early as nine months old and in these cases, a lot of behavioural issues can be managed by taking away the source of frustration or simply moving your baby to another place where he can get on with another activity. A lot of frustration or behavioural issues are borne out of tiredness at this age and as your child gets to two, maybe two and a half years old, much of it is the result of a combination of tiredness and unrealistic expectations about his behaviour.

As parents, you need to communicate with each other so that as your child grows, he will see that you work as a cohesive unit on the issues that matter to you as a family. As a single parent, you should speak to a trusted friend or family member whose parenting style resonates with you. Follow through with what you have committed to at the time, even if later you reconsider the way you reacted. I suggest you consider these points when you think about behaviour and discipline within your family.

1. Is the behaviour worth getting into conflict about – is it worth the battle?
2. Is this about our family values?
3. Is this a social behaviour I/we want to see in our child?

So how do we sort out all of these behaviours?

I find the following method works well with young children as it promotes a two-way solution to behavioural issues. It gives you the chance to be firm with your decisions and gives your child the opportunity to understand why some behaviours are not okay with you.

IGNORE – DISTRACT – REMOVE – DISCIPLINE WITH CONSEQUENCE

IGNORE

Ignoring is best with whingeing behaviour; something that all toddlers and young children can be very adept at! Once the whingeing has stopped, try to distract your child into another activity or a change of scenery. As your child gets older, you can ask her to go to another room until she stops whingeing, at which point she can come to you to talk together about the issue.

DISTRACT

This is the method I use most frequently. The more gently you distract your child, the less she is likely to persist with the behaviour. If you have a biter, watch her closely over a few days and if she looks like she's about to have a nibble on someone, step in and distract her. Distract the baby that's heading for the electrical cords and she will soon forget about pursuing them and move onto something else.

REMOVE

Removing refers to the child or whatever it is that's about to become a missile! Sometimes it's a small child at the end of a meal (remove the food and finish the meal time). If you're in a park, end the play time and take your child home quietly and without fuss. Remember, it's all much easier if there is no shouting from the adults.

DISCIPLINE WITH CONSEQUENCE

Disciplining with consequence is done mostly with older children when you have tried other methods of behaviour management that haven't worked. If you've had a long day with one battle after another, I suggest you sit your child on a step or a chair in a quiet room for three to five minutes. Once she is quiet, you could explain to her that it has been a difficult day and so, tonight, there will be no story before bed. This works well with children between two and three years old. She will still get her kiss and cuddle goodnight, but no story. As your child gets older, the consequence should match the behaviour. Don't threaten anything you aren't prepared to follow through with and, remember, every child is different.

Discipline means you're just putting boundaries around your child's behaviour so that she can cope at a particular age. Keep it age-appropriate and consistent and it will work. The basic rule of thumb is this:

- Under two years of age, ignore, distract, remove.
- As your child gets a bit older, remove and have a conscious consequence.
- When your child is around early school age, you can have a much more complex discussion about discipline. In a very basic form, your message is something like, 'You're getting disciplined for this reason, now I need you to think about what you did.'

- For older primary-aged kids, the message is, 'You've made that decision, you have to live with the consequence' – that's why most kids go into secondary school and have teachers that say, 'If your child doesn't do their homework, don't force them to do it because the consequence is something that will be dealt with at school.' In other words, teaching consequences at a young age is a lesson in fundamental behaviour and one that will have benefits later on.

Calming your child

Try not to reason with your child if she is having a meltdown. She isn't listening to you. Don't try to bribe her into submission either, as this usually backfires and it's a hard habit to break. Instead, try to calm her by using simple phrases, such as 'Calm down, please, Christine' and 'It's time to calm down now.' Repeat this gently until she is quiet and then try to re-engage her to listen to you. Remember to listen to her as well, as she might have a valid point to make! If you expect her to apologise for her behaviour, remember that you need to do the same if your behaviour slips out of control. What she sees is what she learns.

Choices and consequences

Choices are important and therefore so are consequences. If your child never has a consequence, she is never going to really make a choice, is she? The tantrums will just get louder and longer because she doesn't know *why* she needs to stop. If your child is having a tantrum and the only thing she can remember from the last time is that it blew out of control and eventually she got her way, then she will think that must be how she needs to behave again. And believe me, as she gets older, she will get louder, stronger and more wilful.

When I talk about discipline with the parents I see, I tell them that they're setting up their child's moral and social compass and, if the issue is a family value, it's worth the effort. If it's a social behaviour, it's worth the fight too, even if the fight seems miniscule. When you're wondering if it's worth the fight, remember to ask yourself if that is a behaviour you want to see in a child? Do you want to have a child that understands boundaries, so that as she gets older you can talk about those boundaries and they can make sense?

Consistency and predictability

Earlier in this chapter, I mentioned the concept of a child having many carers. It doesn't matter how many people look after your child, it only matters that they are familiar with the way you parent. As for so many aspects of parenting, discipline is rarely going to be completely straightforward. Families are raised in so many ways and in so many different circumstances – the most important thing is that you are in touch with what your child *needs*. Communicate this to other carers and be prepared to make time to talk about issues that arise. Remind each other that the child is exactly that: a child. You are the responsible adults and it is up to you all to create consistent boundaries for that child.

Parents are often at loggerheads about who is doing the disciplining. It's the old 'good cop, bad cop' scenario. Often, the parent who spends the most time with the child is the 'bad cop', while the other parent who comes home at the end of the day (a welcome sight for everyone if it's been hellish) gets a hero's welcome and things can go pear-shaped. It is *really important* for parents to team up. Mums, if you need particular backup, phone your partner and let them know. Your partner is not a mind-reader – you need to communicate. This goes for all the carers in your child's life. If one is dropping the ball, call them on it and sort it out, or weed them out.

When it comes to discipline, one of the strongest messages you can deliver to your child is that his parents are a cohesive team. If your child sees that his parents are supportive of each other in decision-making and discipline and there isn't a crack to wedge into, that sense of togetherness resonates definitively. Parents helping each other in front of their children is something that also creates a very strong impression on kids. Children are a product of their environment and it's up to you, as parents, to create one who is consistent, predictable and appropriate to their age.

31

THE EXPANDING FAMILY

EXPANDING your family is a juggling act and the juggle is about prioritising the needs of a busy family. By busy family, I mean a newborn baby, a two-year-old that needs to go to preschool or day care, and a five-year-old that needs to go to school – plus parents! It's not only about prioritising needs, it's about meeting them as well.

When I see busy families like this, it's usually because the baby's needs have been pushed back and chaos is slowly rearing its head. It's six months since the baby was born and he's up three times at night, doesn't self-settle and sleeps for two twenty-minute sleeps in the day. But everybody else's needs are being met. The toddler is getting to day care, the five-year-old's arrived at school, the uniforms are done and all the after-school activities are being attended.

Over the course of these early months, parents become exhausted and the baby gets lost in the rhythm of the family. Slowly, his needs aren't being met and the only way he can communicate this is by crying, feeding frequently and sleeping very little. Parents will often describe the baby as really happy in the day, even though he is only having two twenty-minute sleeps, and as long as they don't have to put him down. He is fine, as long as the parents are jiggling him consistently until he sleeps in the sling or pram. When it comes to the night, the baby doesn't know how to self-settle and sleep for long periods on his own. Everyone is exhausted.

Unfortunately, I can't turn back the clock but if I could, I would have talked to the parents about priorities and the juggle of family life *before* their baby was born. I would have talked about how much support they have, what they will need to get done in a day and how everyone's needs could be met.

Waiting for the new baby to arrive

Consider the age of your existing children. If you have a toddler (one or more), remember she can't see too far ahead. If you tell her she is going to have a new baby brother soon, she will think it is arriving *today*. It is important to tell siblings the news, but try to hold off until the arrival is closer. If your toddler asks questions, try to answer them honestly. For children under the age of three, the six weeks prior to having the baby is a good time to start talking and getting them ready. You could move beds or rooms, set up the nursery and move car seats – all visual things that will signal change is about to happen. Often the younger children have not spent too much time apart from their parents so now is a good time to take

223

them for a visit to the hospital and explain that this is where mum will be having the baby. If you show your younger children photos of them as babies in hospital with you, they can visualise and understand that you will be there for a few days with their new baby brother or sister too.

In hospital

In terms of introducing a new baby to young children, there's no need to overthink it. You just need to make things as 'normal' as you can. Short visits are better for toddlers as too much time in small spaces can easily lead to destruction! Mornings are better as they're unlikely to be too tired and can be easily distracted when it's time to leave. It's often an emotional time for parents who are excited about the new baby but are now seeing that the older child or children seem much older and more grown up.

Let your children get to know the new baby. If the baby is feeding, explain this to the siblings and use the time to talk and answer their questions. If siblings are very young and all they hear is 'NO' and 'DON'T', they will instinctively want to find out more and try to hit or poke the baby. Once a feed is finished, lie the baby on a blanket and let his siblings gently touch him (with clean hands). It is unlikely they will hurt their new brother, and often will be more willing to leave the baby after a little 'dose'! If the baby is asleep, explain that you need to leave him be for a while and take the opportunity to spend time with your older children. It's a good idea to have something else for your children to do while they're visiting. Pack a couple of puzzles into your hospital bag.

When you're in hospital, remember that this is precious time to spend with your new baby before you go home. It's a good time to get to know each other because when you do get home, alone time together is rare and often only in the quiet of night when everyone else is sleeping. Enjoy the time together.

Siblings

Your older children will generally be excited about the new baby but are likely to react differently. You just need to be patient as they adjust to a new rhythm in the house.

TODDLERS

Most toddlers are kind and gentle with their new baby brother or sister. It is important, however, to be mindful that a new baby can be hardest on this age group since they are the centre of their own world and dislike being disrupted. Try to keep things going as normally as possible with day care, preschool and/or other activities. It helps to keep drop-off and pick-up times as familiar as possible too. Let family and friends help by watching the new baby or doing the running around for you. If your toddler isn't getting what she needs from you, she will let you know. The most important thing is to resist blaming the new baby for your toddler's behaviour. It's also vital that you spend some one-on-one time with your toddler whenever you possibly can.

Parents are often concerned about the baby waking the older children during the night. This rarely happens but if it does, particularly around four or five o'clock in the morning, most siblings will go back to sleep after reassurance.

Before you feed your baby, set up an activity for your toddler to do. It might be tricky, but try not to be distracted from the baby's feed as this is likely to lead to snack feeding and, in turn, more frequent feeds. Obviously, the safety of your toddler is paramount, so remove any likelihood of danger and focus on encouraging a good feed for your baby. You might feel like you are using the television a lot but as your baby settles into feeding regularly your toddler will understand that watching television is just while the baby is feeding.

OLDER SIBLINGS

Older children are usually very excited about the arrival of a new baby and, depending on their age, they can be very helpful! The great thing about older children is they can let you know if something is not working for them. They can also understand you when you explain how you looked after them when they were babies and that you had to spend a lot of time together with them too. Show them photos again and, if they are old enough, get them involved with the baby. They can get and hold things for you, such as nappies and wraps, and usually love to be asked to help.

The important thing to notice about older siblings is if they start to go quiet. It usually means they've been so good you've missed the great things they are doing. This can be hard for a young child so make sure you spend a bit of time each day to talk about what they're doing and how much you appreciate them.

It's okay to say no

There is a lot of pressure on parents to provide endless activities for their older children, but actually, it's okay to say no to this. For the first three months of the baby's life, the five-year-old can just go to school and come home. If the toddler is going to day care, it's okay to drop off a little late and pick up a little early if it means making your family life run smoothly. For older siblings, cutting back on activities is not a bad idea. The cost of not doing this is usually a very unsettled baby. Explain to your children that cutting back isn't forever and it's part of sharing life as a family when the baby is very young.

When I'm lucky enough to see parents before their baby is born, I always have the discussion about priorities. I suggest they get their friends to help out, particularly if there is more than one school or day care drop-off and pick-up. I encourage them to think carefully about what they really can and can't manage. It's hard to be too prescriptive in a book about this topic, because it really is a conversation about the priorities of all members of the family. You need to have this conversation with the people that are going to be able to help you. It might be with your favourite mothercraft nurse, your mother or your close friends, but it's definitely worth thinking about ahead of the arrival.

So whether you employ someone to help, you have parents who are willing and able, or you have a sister, neighbour or friends, look at where that help will actually work for you. Working out the help that you need is about listing everyone in your family, what they need and when. It can be as simple as drawing up a chart and filling in the gaps.

Simplifying needs

A child's life is slow and methodical. It just wanders along, one minute playing with Lego, the next minute jumping in puddles. Simplifying the family's lives to cope with the needs of the new baby is part of family life. It is worthwhile making those compromises when you see your calm and happy baby growing into your family. The first six months go by very quickly so, for the sake of your whole family, slow things down and the juggle will be infinitely easier to manage.

Looking after yourselves

As with much of family life, parents tend to put their own needs at the end of the priority list. It's important for you to connect with your partner, or with other adults, even if it's only for short windows of time. Making time to do this will make a huge difference to you as you juggle the demands of family life.

REMEMBER ...

- Sleep is important for you – it's important to rest when you can – even a twenty minute nap makes a difference.
- Ask for help – sharing pick-ups and drop-offs of other children for the first six weeks is a huge help.
- Ask family and friends to bring meals and do small amounts of shopping.
- Eat well and exercise, even if it's just a walk with the baby in the pram.
- Set realistic ideals about what you can do – it will decrease stress and make parenting far more enjoyable.

32

TRAVEL

YOU should never hesitate to travel with your baby but you should make sure you plan carefully. Some parents are so daunted by the idea of travelling with children, regardless of whether it's from Sydney to Brisbane or whether it's to the other side of the world, they don't think about it before they get on a flight. There's a lot to be said for keeping an open mind while travelling but when you have children, you need to plan, plan, plan.

The first things you need to consider are the age of your child, where you're going and what you're doing. Anyone under two years old isn't really going on a holiday, they've just changed house for a while. If you think you're going to trip around the ruins of Rome with a one-year-old, I'd suggest it will be a very stressful holiday for everybody. It doesn't mean you can't go to Rome, you just need to plan it differently.

Regardless of whether you're planning a trip overseas or an hour's drive up the coast, you need to be aware that if you have young children, the only thing that matters to them is having their needs met.

Chaos v calm

If you're going to travel overseas, let's say to the northern hemisphere, I think you have to go for at least two weeks. Anything less is a lot of hard work and you just end up with compacted jet lag. The other major issue you need to try to avoid is moving all the time. Try to base yourselves in no more than two or three places over the two weeks, as it's difficult for children when their environment is constantly changing.

I work with a lot of families that have extended family overseas. Christmas time can be hard for your child if you are constantly doing all the visiting while you're away. You're better off telling family you are going to be based in one or two places and for them to visit you. You can enjoy the company of your overseas family while you and your child stay in as stable a rhythm as possible. Everyone has a much better time.

Sleeping child on a flight = bliss

There are those babies that fit into the airline-issued bassinette and those that don't. If your baby fits into the bassinette, pack an extra small cotton blanket to drape over part of the top of the bassinette. Using masking tape to stick it to the wall helps you to adjust it perfectly over the bassinette as well. This will block out the light, especially on day flights where it comes in at all angles. Lightly wrap your baby's arms in as they often hit the sides of the bassinette as he sleeps.

If you have an older child that is sitting on your lap for the flight, sleeping can be a bit trickier. It might be cheaper to go without a dedicated seat for him, but even on a short flight this can be hard. There is a lot more stimulation on a flight and if your child is used to sleeping in a bed, sitting on your lap creates a lot less space to stretch out. You'll need a bit of patience. Use the light blanket over your child's shoulders to create a quiet and less stimulated environment and stay nice and calm.

Making up bottles on a flight

On a long-haul flight, you need to feed fluids to your baby about every three hours with one six-hour break towards the end. Flying is dehydrating at the best of times so make sure you keep your fluids up as well, particularly if you are breastfeeding. Make a point of drinking a good amount of water every time you feed your baby.

Aviation security requirements restrict the amount of water you can take onto a flight. If you take bottles containing made-up formula on a flight, airport security will ask you to taste each bottle. On a long-haul flight that can mean six or seven bottles so that's also a lot of weight to carry. Neither situation is ideal.

A better way to manage bottlefeeding on a flight is as follows:
1. Take the number of bottles that you need and the formula amounts in a formula dispenser plus one for emergencies (in case you have flight delays or a spillage).
2. When a feed is due, ask the flight staff to fill the bottle with two-thirds cold water and one-third boiling water.

3. Add the formula yourself and shake well for the feed.
4. After the feed, ask the flight staff to rinse the bottle in hot water.
5. Turn the teat inside the bottle so you know that you have used that bottle.

You can take sealed tins of formula into countries in your baggage but, depending on security restrictions in other countries, any open tins may need to be thrown out. Contact the manufacturer of your baby formula to see what they have available at your destination.

Jet lag

Adjusting to new time zones needn't be as hard as you think. If you are going on a long-haul flight, you need to accept that there is going to be a period of adjustment and allow for it when you land.

Think ahead about jet lag. Regardless of how long the flight is, your baby or young child needs to adjust to the time on the ground from the moment you land. So if you land at two o'clock in the afternoon, you need to pick up the day from that point, which would be hard if they have just been sleeping for the past six hours. If your child normally has dinner at five o'clock, then give her dinner at five o'clock at the local time. Sunlight helps to regulate day/night patterns so the more night flights you can arrange, the better. If you're flying to the northern hemisphere, a longer first leg gives you and your child a better chance of getting a decent rest on the flight.

Accommodation

Travelling is expensive, I realise this. But I do suggest you try to factor in some inevitabilities into your journey, such as your child's need for sleep during the day and early nights to bed. If you book one room in a beautiful hotel and you have a one-year-old baby, you are going to have to think about how your baby's sleep is going to pan out. He will still need a morning and afternoon sleep, though you can get away with giving him his morning sleep in a pram or a car. If you give him the chance to have a good afternoon sleep in bed, you've got more chance of going out for dinners without a cranky child. How are you going to do this? Are you all going to be sitting cross-legged in the hallway while the one-year-old sleeps in the room? And what is going to happen at seven o'clock at night when your one-year-old needs to go to sleep – in the dark? You will either need to get a bigger room with a bigger bathroom for a portable cot (don't laugh, it's the perfect solution) or you'll need to get connecting rooms or a one-bedroom suite. So yes, travelling with a family is expensive but there are lots of alternatives to costly hotels – seek them out.

Toddlers and travel . . . hmmm

Think very carefully about putting a child aged between fourteen months and two years on a long-haul flight – actually any flight. At this age, a child's whole purpose for existence is to walk and move, walk and move, walk and move or jump, jump, jump, jump, jump. If you absolutely need to fly, definitely book the night flights because, at the very least, you will get a break while your toddler sleeps.

There are little tricks that I've learned over the years that make travelling so much easier. Preparing for flights and packing for holidays is second nature to me now. I pack exactly the same amount going to Hamilton Island for a week as I would going to Europe for three weeks. If you're visiting family overseas, ask them to do a shop for nappies and other basics. There are places where you can hire a cot, high chair, car seat, pram – pretty much anything you need – and they will meet you at the airport with all the gear (or get it delivered to wherever you're staying). You can also go online to the nearest supermarket and have a food delivery made to the apartment you're renting or to the house you're staying in. It just takes planning and a bit of ingenuity in working out what you need.

Travel tips
- Try to book flights with airlines that offer prams for your use at the airport.
- Remember to take food and snacks (and remember to throw them out before you land).
- Allow for a bit of extra time at the airport before you leave.
- Put your young baby in an all-in-one suit for the flight as it can get cold in the cabin.

Packing for the flight
- 6–8 nappies
- Wipes
- Change mat
- Nappy disposal bags
- 3–4 bibs

- Extra set of clothes
- Wrap
- Light cotton blanket + a small roll of masking tape
- Comforter
- Dummies + dummy chain

The packing list for your luggage

- Packet of nappies (nappies are pretty much the same all over the world)
- Packet of wipes
- 4 singlets
- 2 pairs of pyjamas
- 3 sets of bottoms (short or long, depending on where you're going)
- 5 tops
- 2 good outfits
- Socks, shoes, hats
- Swimwear if you need it
- Bottles if needed
- Formula
- Formula dispenser
- Portacot cover (new on the market and very handy)
- Block-out curtain with suction caps
- Infant paracetamol or ibuprofen

Travelling with your young family is a memory-making experience. Whether everything seems to go wrong or the trip goes off without a hitch, it will be an adventure, just as family life is. And just as it is with travel, family life will serve you with good days and bad days. But know this: it goes *very quickly* so make every day count. Nurture your kids and accept them for who they are. The patience, consistency and love you give your children in these early days will enrich your family for its exciting journey ahead.

RESOURCES

FIRST-AID COURSES
www.stjohn.org.au – St John First-Aid courses
www.cprkids.com.au – Child-specific CPR and first-aid
    courses

HEALTH & SAFETY
Poisons Information Centre 131126
Vaccination Information Service 9144 6625

LOOKING AFTER YOURSELF
www.beyondblue.com.au – Raising awareness of and help for
    those suffering from anxiety and depression
www.gidgetfoundation.com.au – Raising awareness of
    perinatal (pre- and post-natal) anxiety and depression

SLEEPING

www.sidsandkids.org – Safe sleeping information

www.safesleepspace.com.au – Strategies and help with sleep
from Helen Stevens

www.tresillian.net – Parenting support and advice

www.karitane.com.au – Parenting support and advice

CLOTHING

www.cancercouncil.com.au – Protective clothing and
sunscreen

FEEDING

www.breastfeeding.asn.au – Australian Breastfeeding
Association

www.speechpathologyservices.com.au – Information
on introducing solids from Dr Sarah Starr, speech
pathologist

www.louisefultonkeats.com – Delicious family food recipes
from Louise Fulton Keats

www.annabelkarmel.com – Recipes and fun food ideas for
babies and toddlers from Annabel Karmel

CAR SAFETY

www.roadsafety.transport.nsw.gov.au/stayingsafe/children/
childcarseats/ – Australia's National Child Restraint Laws

www.acri.com.au – Australian Child Restraint Resource
Initiative – list of accredited child-restraint providers and
installers

SURROGACY

www.fertilityconnections.com.au – Altruistic surrogacy information

www.immi.gov.au/media/fact-sheets/36a_surrogacy. htm – Surrogacy laws in Australia

GRANDPARENTING

www.chw.edu.au – Child health and parenting information from the Children's Hospital, Westmead, for health professionals and parents

www.accc.gov.au – Cot safety guidelines

www.raisingchildren.net.au – Comprehensive, practical, expert information on child health and parenting + activities for children 0–8 years

www.playgroupaustralia.org.au – Online directory of playgroups available across Australia

www.grandparents.about.com – Discussion and resources for grandparents

PREMATURE BABIES

www.prembaby.org.au – Information point for organisations supporting parents of premature babies

www.bornearly.com.au – Information about National Premature Birth Awareness Week

www.austprem.org.au – Forums and support for parents of premature babies

MULTIPLES

www.thinktwins.com.au – Products and resources for families with twins

www.amba.org.au – Australian Multiple Birth
Association – support and information for families with
twins and more

TOILET TRAINING
www.brollysheets.com.au – Excellent for toilet training

OTHER FAVOURITE SITES for handy items, advice and support to help with raising your kids
www.haggusandstookles.com.au
www.plumcollections.com.au
www.urbanbaby.com.au
www.babyology.com.au
www.kinderling.com.au
www.essentialbaby.com.au

CHEAT SHEETS

The cheat sheets that follow have been left
blank for you to complete for your own child.

CHEAT SHEET: SOLIDS

THE BASICS . . .

SUGGESTIONS FOR YOUR BABY'S FIRST MEALS

FIRST DAY AND THEN DAILY FOR 2–3 DAYS

2–3 DAYS LATER

2–3 DAYS LATER

2–3 DAYS LATER

2–3 DAYS LATER

THINGS TO NOTE . . .

CHEAT SHEET:
BIRTH TO 3 WEEKS

THINGS TO CONSIDER

SLEEP

SETTLING

WHAT DO BABIES NEED AT THIS AGE?

RHYTHMIC PATTERN

TIPS FOR PARENTS OF NEWBORNS

CHEAT SHEET:
3–6 WEEKS

THINGS TO CONSIDER

FEEDING

SLEEP

SETTLING

WHAT DO BABIES NEED AT THIS AGE?

FEEDING

SLEEP

RHYTHMIC PATTERN

SUGGESTED DAILY RHYTHM

MORNING FEED

MID-MORNING FEED

LUNCH-TIME FEED

AFTERNOON FEED

EVENING FEED

OVERNIGHT

CHEAT SHEET:
6–12 WEEKS

THINGS TO CONSIDER

SLEEP

SETTLING

SUGGESTED DAILY RHYTHM AT 6 WEEKS

WHAT DO BABIES NEED AT THIS AGE?

SLEEP

RHYTHMIC PATTERN

SUGGESTED DAILY RHYTHM AT 12 WEEKS

CHEAT SHEET: 3–6 MONTHS

3 MONTHS

FEEDING

SLEEP

SUGGESTED DAILY RHYTHM

5 MONTHS

FEEDING

SLEEP

SUGGESTED DAILY RHYTHM

6 MONTHS

FEEDING

SLEEP

SUGGESTED DAILY RHYTHM

CHEAT SHEET: 6–9 MONTHS

6 MONTHS

FEEDING

SLEEPING

DEVELOPMENT

SUGGESTED DAILY RHYTHM

7 MONTHS

FEEDING

SLEEPING

DEVELOPMENT

SUGGESTED DAILY RHYTHM

8 MONTHS

FEEDING

SLEEPING

DEVELOPMENT

SUGGESTED DAILY RHYTHM

CHEAT SHEET:
9–12 MONTHS

WHAT TO EXPECT

9 MONTHS

FEEDING

SUGGESTED DAILY RHYTHM

12 MONTHS

FEEDING

CHEAT SHEET:
12–18 MONTHS

14 MONTHS

FEEDING

SUGGESTED DAILY RHYTHM

16 MONTHS

FEEDING

SUGGESTED DAILY RHYTHM

18 MONTHS

FEEDING

SUGGESTED DAILY RHYTHM

ACKNOWLEDGEMENTS

There are two people I especially wish to thank for their help during this process, who both believed in me and saw a book inside me before I did.

Firstly, Alex Craig, for encouraging me to believe that what I say to parents at home with young children was valuable enough to share.

And Sally Murray, for all the time, effort and many, many hours of laughter – your talent for turning my thoughts into words is immense and I am so grateful for the friendship that has developed along the way. My very humble thanks.

INDEX